She Believed God, So She Moved

The Faith- Fueled Guide to Peace, Purpose, and Progress

By. Shaasia Nance

Godly Beauty Publishing

Copyright © 2025 by Shaasia Nance

Published by Godly Beauty Publishing
www.urgodlybeauty.com

ISBN: 979-8-9930090-0-1 (Paperback)
ISBN: 979-8-9930090-1-8 (E-book)

Cover design by Tanesha Berry
Interior design by Godly Beauty Publishing

All Scripture quotations are taken from the King James Version of the Bible. Public domain.

All rights reserved. No part of this publication may be reproduced, stored in a retrieval system, or transmitted in any form or by any means, including electronic, mechanical, photocopying, recording, or otherwise, without prior written permission of the publisher and copyright owners.

The use of short quotations or the copying of an occasional page for personal or group discussion study is permitted and encouraged. Permission will be granted upon request. For permission, please contact:
info@urgodlybeauty.com

The examples used in this book are compilations of stories from real situations. In select situations, names, facts, and issues have been altered to protect confidentiality while illustrating the points. The ideas, suggestions, general principles, and conclusions presented here reflect the views of the author, and your implementation of the information provided should be adapted to fit your own particular situation or circumstance.

The author has made every effort to ensure the accuracy of the information herein. However, the information contained in this book is provided without warranty, either express or implied. While the author has made every effort to provide accurate internet addresses at the time of publication, neither the publisher nor the author assumes any responsibility for errors or for changes that occur after publication.
First Edition
Printed in the United States of America

PREFACE

I didn't always move when God said move. There were seasons when fear held my feet hostage. When the opinions of others drowned out God's voice. When I believed more in my own limitations than in the limitless power of the One who called me. But something shifted when I stopped rehearsing my insecurities and started rehearsing His promises.

She Believed God, So She Moved was birthed from that shift.

This book is more than a message, it's a movement. A bold, faith-filled invitation for women like you, who are tired of standing still in places God never meant for you to camp. It's for the ones who know they were made for more but just need the courage to step out of the boat.

Inside these pages, I share what God taught me about obedience, identity, boldness, and breakthrough. I wrote this for the woman who feels called but unqualified. For the woman who wants to move but isn't sure how. For the woman who's ready to break agreement with fear and step into faith like never before.

My prayer is that every word in this book stirs your spirit, ignites your confidence, and reminds you: when you truly believe God, you won't just dream, you'll move. Let's walk it out together.

With expectancy and grace,
Shaasia Nance,
The MEGA Overload Coach

Table of Contents

Part One: Purpose
Chapter 1   Discovering Your Purpose is the First Step to Unlocking the Life You Were Created to Live 3
Chapter 2   Embracing Your Purpose is How You Move from Confusion to Clarity and Confidence 35
Chapter 3   Thriving in Your Purpose Happens When You Fully Align Your Faith, Gifts, and Daily Actions 57

Part Two: Ladder
Chapter 4   Positioning Your Ladder Is the Key to Making Sure You're Climbing Toward Purpose, Not Just Success 73
Chapter 5   Being Diligent on Your Ladder Means Staying Focused, Faithful, and Fruitful No Matter the Level You're On 83

Part Three: Affirming
Chapter 6   Affirming Yourself in God's Word Is How You Replace Self-Doubt with Unshakable Identity and Confidence 95

Part Four: Intentionality
Chapter 7   Being Obedient Through Intentionality Is How You Turn Daily Decisions Into Divine Alignment 117

Part Five: Nurturing
Chapter 8   Surrounding Yourself with Nurturers Is How You Grow Faster, Heal Deeper, and Rise Stronger 137

Forward

For one full year my wife went on a remarkable journey. As her husband, I had the privilege of watching her begin and faithfully walk this path. Whenever you see someone step into a journey that seems long and challenging, you naturally wonder how they will endure it and what lasting impact it will leave on their life. I witnessed firsthand the transformation that took place in my wife as she pressed forward, and this book is the fruit of that journey.

From a young age, her life has been dedicated to pursuing Christ. She has carried a passion not only to know God more intimately but also to help others cultivate a deeper, personal relationship with Him. Her focus has always been to remove distractions and interference, creating a clear path of open communication with God so His purpose and plans can be revealed. She is a living example of what God can do when we take off the limitations and allow Him to have His way.

This book is the result: a framework that, with prayer, labor, and perseverance, will open your eyes to see your destiny. It is not just an idea but a tried and proven method to define purpose, illuminate a path, and lead to fulfillment. The method is truly PLAIN. If you follow the steps, press through the uncomfortable moments, move beyond worry and doubt, and rely fully on God for strength, you will begin to see the beauty of His purpose in your life, your talents, and your calling.

My wife has been an inspiration to me in my own Christian walk, and I know she will inspire you as well. This book was written through her by divine inspiration. It is more than a book; it is a movement. And movement requires moving. Allow yourself to be moved, because this Spirit-inspired work will do exactly that.

— RC

First, I give all glory, honor, and praise to my Heavenly Father, my Lord and Savior Jesus Christ, and the Holy Spirit. Without His grace, wisdom, and strength, this book would not exist.

To my husband Ron, my partner, best friend, and greatest blessing, thank you for standing with me in every season. To my precious children, you are my joy and my inspiration to leave a legacy of faith and purpose.

To my mother, whose unwavering love, steadfast faith, and powerful prayers have carried me farther than words can say. To my brother Marquel, my real-life hero, whose strength and example inspire me daily. To my nana, whose wisdom has guided me; my uncles, who have always stood by me with love and support; and my in-laws, Pastors Ronald and Rose, whose faith and inspiration encourage me to walk boldly in my calling.

To my cherished friend MaLisha, who has walked with me through challenges and celebrated every victory; my mentor Charmayne, for her invaluable wisdom and guidance; my amazing friend Shayla, whose support has uplifted me through the years; my sister Courtney, who has shared with me laughter that made us cry and tears that led us to prayer; my dear friend Kiara, whose kindness has been a quiet strength; and Aunt Juanita, whose constant cheering has been a reminder of God's goodness.

Finally, this book is dedicated to every woman who has ever questioned her worth. May you be reminded that you are fearfully and wonderfully made, created with purpose, and called to live boldly in Christ.

INTRODUCTION

Imagine a woman of faith. Committed. Determined. Deeply in love with God. She is navigating life with the best of intentions, but without clear direction from God. She works hard, overextends herself, and says yes to every opportunity, hoping her effort will prove her devotion. She confuses movement with momentum and assumes that busyness equals obedience. She pours out for everyone else while quietly running on empty. Her heart is sincere, but her strategy is scattered.

One day, in a moment of complete exhaustion, she falls to her knees and cries out, "God, is this really what You called me to? There has to be more than this." Then, God responds.

"Pray and seek Me daily for one full year. Make Me your first focus every morning. Ask Me to reveal your kingdom assignment every single day." That simple but specific instruction became the catalyst for her supernatural clarity.

As she obeyed, God began to download a framework, not just for daily purpose, but for divine alignment. A pattern. A pathway. A plan. He called it *PLAIN* Vision.

Over the course of that one year, everything began to shift. Her confusion turned into clarity. Her striving turned into strategy. Her burnout transformed into overflow. That woman was me.

My name is Shaasia Nance, and I want to show you what God showed me. What He did in my life, I truly believe He can do in yours. Because here is the truth: we are all being pulled by families, careers, ministries, dreams, and expectations. But beneath all the noise, there is a divine tug calling you deeper. There is a kingdom assignment with your name on it. God does not just want you busy. He wants you aligned.

If you have been feeling overwhelmed, unfocused, or unsure of what is next, I invite you to step into the same process that changed my life. Let us take everything you are doing and bring it into divine order. Let us go from pressure to purpose. Let us walk in PLAIN Vision.

This book is your invitation to live from overflow, not by chance but by choice, not in confusion but with clarity, not in reaction but with revelation. It is a call to step into your God-given purpose by not only listening to His voice but also acting on His direction with intentionality.

Inside these pages, you will discover the *PLAIN* Vision framework that will sharpen your focus, giving you the ability to lead your life, not follow it. You will exchange chaos for clarity and busyness for breakthrough.

Ask yourself: Are you ready to move? If so, believe that God will meet you right where you are. He is ready to lead you, shape you, and walk with you as you step fully into the life He strategically designed just for you.

It's time to pray strategically, plan prophetically, and pursue purpose intentionally.

Welcome to the journey. Let's move.

In this season, God is not just calling you to purpose. He is commanding you to execute with precision. It is not enough to dream. It is not enough to wish. It is time to build with clarity, to walk in divine alignment, and to live with intention.

This is your PLAIN Vision.

"Write the vision, and make it plain upon tables, that he may run that readeth it."

—Habakkuk 2:2

God is not giving you a foggy future. He is giving you a clear blueprint, a strategy, a system, and a prophetic path. Let us break it down.

God's plans for your life are not passive. They require your active participation through prayer, discernment, and goal setting that reflects His purpose. To help you do this, we will explore a process I call *PLAIN* Vision. *PLAIN* is an acronym for the framework that will guide you in discovering and living out God's purpose for you.

P = Purpose

Your purpose is not random. It is divinely designed. It is the fire in your bones, the pull in your spirit, and the whisper that wakes you up at night. It is the reason you were born. Purpose is the revelation of why God placed you into the earth. Your dreams and desires are not accidents. They are divine echoes of God's intent for your life. When you unlock your purpose, you unlock the first key to your assignment.

L = Ladder

You cannot fly without a foundation. Destiny is climbed, not jumped. Each rung on the ladder represents a step in your process. You cannot skip development and expect elevation. God is not only calling you to the promise, He is calling you to the process. Every step matters, and every act of obedience builds spiritual muscle. This is your call to climb, rung by rung, toward your next level.

A = Affirmation

God speaks over you, and now it is time to echo back what He has already said. Affirmations are not cute quotes or trendy declarations. They are spiritual warfare tools. They are seeds of growth and encouragement that help combat negative ideas the enemy uses to undermine your sense of self-worth. Affirmations uproot the lies of the enemy and reinforce your God-given identity. Understand this: your words are powerful. You will eat the fruit of your lips. So speak life, speak purpose, and speak power.

When you speak in alignment with God's Word, you shift atmospheres, rewire your thinking, and fortify your faith.

I = Intentionality

Nothing about your destiny is accidental. Obedience begins with intentionality. It is how you honor the prophetic words spoken over your life by turning them into obedient action. Intentional living is how you steward your time, your energy, and your priorities, not by acci dent, but by assignment. When you live with intention, you live in obedience. You partner with the Holy Spirit not just by hearing His voice, but by responding to it. Intentionality is obedience in motion. No more random living. No more drifting. It is time to move with Spirit-led precision, disciplined devotion, and bold surrender.

N = *Nurture*

You were never meant to grow in isolation. Nurturing your purpose means surrounding yourself with divine connections. These are people who challenge you, push you, intercede for you, and speak to the future in you. This is the season for pruning relationships that drain and embracing relationships that grow. Iron sharpeneth iron. Find your tribe. Find your midwives. Find your intercessors. You cannot fulfill a God-sized vision without a God-ordained circle.

As you read this book, we will explore what it means to follow God's will, how to discern His guidance, and how to turn that guidance into tangible goals. You will discover practical steps for staying on track when challenges arise and learn how to balance faith with action in a way that honors God. Through prayer, discernment, and focused action, you will move from overwhelmed to aligned, from busy to purposeful, and from striving to surrendered living.

If you have ever felt the pull between your personal dreams and God's calling, this journey is for you. It is time to step boldly into your calling and watch God transform your path as you follow through. It is time to stop just dreaming and start making that dream a reality by allowing God to make the vision *PLAIN*.

PART 1: PURPOSE

Purpose is not just a concept. It is a divine force. It is the spiritual engine that powers your growth, fuels your drive, and gives your existence eternal weight. When you walk in purpose, you are not merely living. You are aligning with God's intention for your life.

You were not born to drift. You were born to dominate.

Purpose is the reason behind your breath. It is the "why" behind every meaningful action, the compass that governs your decisions, and the fire that ignites your passion to impact the world for the glory of God. Purpose is not optional. It is essential.

When purpose is activated, confusion breaks. When purpose is clear, destiny accelerates. It is what causes you to say no to distractions and yes to divine assignments.

Purpose is not passive. Rather, it is the divine mission coded into your spirit before you were ever formed in your mother's womb. It is what pulls you forward when you feel stuck. It is what whispers, "There is more," when everything around you says, "Settle."

Purpose is both the path and the power. It is the divine design behind your goals, your dreams, your burdens, and your callings. It manifests in many forms:

A mission that drives you
A function you were created to fulfill
A destiny you are anointed to walk out
A divine target you are graced to hit

Call it what you will. Your objective, your assignment, your calling, your design. But understand this: your purpose is Heaven's investment in you. And God expects a return.

"For we are his workmanship, created in Christ Jesus unto good works, which God hath before ordained that we should walk in them."

—Ephesians 2:10

Now is the time to stop wandering and start walking in divine direction. You were created on purpose, with purpose, for a purpose, because of His purpose.

Let us uncover it. Let us unlock it. Let us ignite it.

CHAPTER 1: THE JOURNEY BEGINS: DISCOVERING YOUR UNIQUE GIFTS AND PASSIONS

"You must know Him to know yourself, and only then will you know what you were created to do."

-Shaasia Nance

As you embark on this divine journey of self-discovery, understand this: You were fearfully and wonderfully made, not just to exist, but to impact, to build, to reign. You are not a coincidence. You are not random. You are God's intentional design, crafted with precision, endowed with gifts. Heaven has deposited within you a constellation of gifts, passions, and experiences that point directly to your God-ordained assignment. Your uniqueness is not an afterthought, it is your superpower.

Take the time to think about the things that light you up inside. What are you passionate about? What brings you joy and fulfillment? Maybe it is writing, painting, singing, or helping others in need. Whatever it is, pay attention to those passions. These are not passing interests, they are clues. God uses your passion as a compass to guide you into purpose.

"I will praise thee; for I am fearfully and wonderfully made: marvellous are thy works; and that my soul knoweth right well."

—Psalm 139:14

You are the handiwork of God. The very breath of the Creator flows through your being. Just as a parent sees their reflection in the face of their child, you are a reflection of your Heavenly Father. Every gift, every talent, every characteristic in you is divine DNA, designed with kingdom purpose in mind.

Let me be clear: You carry something no one else can duplicate. The oil on your life, the anointing on your voice, the wisdom in your story, it cannot be imitated. God has placed within you a mantle, a mission, a message that only you can carry. And it is that uniqueness which positions you to transform the world around you.

Think of Queen Esther. She did not rise to royalty by chance. Her story was laced with pain, displacement, and pressure. But her uniqueness, her strength, her beauty, and her boldness, was the very thing God used to position her for divine influence. Esther was handpicked, divinely aligned, and supernaturally equipped for such a time as this.

So are you.

Every test, every loss, every moment that felt like delay was actually divine preparation. Your experiences are the soil where your purpose takes root. They were never meant to bury you, they were meant to birth you.

Remember this:
You are not waiting to be called, you have already been chosen.
You are not average, you are appointed.
You are not replaceable, you are irreplaceable.

There is only one you walking this earth. Others may try to imitate your style, mimic your sound, or replicate your rhythm, but they will never carry your oil. What God has placed in you is sacred, strategic, and sealed for your destiny.
Let this be your declaration:

"I am uniquely anointed. I am divinely appointed. I will discover, develop, and deploy every gift God has placed inside of me."

Now rise up, daughter of destiny. This is the beginning of your unveiling. The world is waiting for what only you carry.

Are You Willing to Be Developed in the Field?

Have you ever stood in the middle of a storm, praying, pleading, even fasting, asking God to move a problem out of your way, only to find that it remains? You begin to wonder, "God, where are You? Why haven't You changed this yet?" I've asked those same questions. But what I've come to realize is this: The obstacles you often ask God to remove are actually divine stages, strategically set to reveal the strength He has deposited within you.

Hear me clearly, your problem is not punishment; it is preparation. You have been equipped for this. That battle you're facing right now? You didn't stumble into it; you were summoned. You were handpicked by Heaven to stand, to speak, to fight, and to overcome.

There will come a moment, if it hasn't already, where a challenge presents itself that looks eerily familiar. Yet it is heavier, deeper, and more complex than before. Just like David facing Goliath, you'll realize this battle has your name on it. Why? Because you're the only one equipped to take it down.

Let's revisit the story of David. Not as king, but the overlooked shepherd. While his brothers were paraded in front of the prophet Samuel, David was hidden in the fields. Not forgotten by God, but formed by Him. While tending sheep, David wasn't just passing time; he was learning to war in obscurity. He was being taught to fight lions and bears, to worship in the wild, and to lead without recognition. What looked like rejection was actually divine redirection.

Don't miss this: Jesse did not invite David to the sacrifice because he did not see him as worthy, God created the entire event just to reveal him. Sometimes, those closest to you will underestimate your worth, but God will elevate you in front of the very ones who overlooked you. The space others try to exclude you from, God will tailor it to fit your anointing.

Where Jesse saw a shepherd, God saw a king.
Where man saw insignificance, God saw a solution.

Let me speak this truth into your spirit. No one can cancel what Heaven has confirmed. They can't close the door on your destiny. They didn't open it, and they can't shut it. Only you can disqualify yourself by not showing up.

God is saying to you today:
Show up.
Show up in faith.
Show up with your sling.
Show up with your scars and your story.
Show up, because He has already gone before you.

When David stood before Goliath, it wasn't just about a stone; it was about stewardship. He had already proven faithful with sheep, and now he was prepared to lead a nation. That one victory unlocked his next level, and it didn't stop there. David didn't just become a warrior. He became a psalmist, prophet, worship leader, husband, father, king, and legacy builder. As he unlocked his gifts, his roles multiplied. And so will yours.

As you move forward boldly, prophetically, and obediently, you will uncover new dimensions of your identity, new depths of your purpose, and new rooms of influence you never knew existed. The oil on your life will begin to flow in arenas you never imagined.

So I ask you:
Are you willing to be developed in the field before being revealed in the palace?
Are you ready to stop asking for the mountain to move and start climbing it with the tools God has given you?
Are you prepared to walk in the fullness of who God says you are, even when others don't recognize it? Because if you are, get ready.

The same God who saw David in the pasture is watching you now.

He has called you. He has equipped you. And He will perform His Word concerning you. All you have to do is show up.

My Testimony: He Had a Plan All Along

When I was in the first grade, I got into trouble not for being disruptive or disrespectful, but for stealing. Yes, stealing. I was captivated by my teacher's desk, the colorful pens, the stamps, the stickers, the grade book. I would sneak those items into my bookbag, take them home, and transform my bedroom into a full-fledged classroom. I'd line my cousins up like students, write lessons on the wall, and grade pretend papers like my life depended on it. And in a very real sense, it did.

To the school, I was stealing.
To my mother, I was being disobedient.
But to God? I was already walking in my calling.

Back then, we didn't know what to make of it. I wasn't a rebellious child. In fact, that was the most trouble I ever got into as a kid. My mom would discipline me, but I couldn't explain it. There was just something about teaching that I couldn't stay away from. Eventually, she started buying me my own teacher tools, and I learned to ask instead of take. But the fascination never left.

Years later, my pastor stood in the pulpit and released a word that would change everything. "God places gifts, skills, and divine desires in you at a young age. If you want to know your purpose, look back at what you loved as a child." At that moment, I saw it clearly. I was always a teacher. I was always called to lead, to instruct, to ignite the minds and spirits of others.

At that moment, everything clicked. I sat in church thinking: That was me. That was teaching. That was purpose speaking before I had the words to explain it. Now, teaching is not just my profession. It is my assignment. It is what God wired me for before I ever knew what a calling was. And here's what I've learned: Purpose often shows up in childhood, but it takes time to recognize.

God will use the very things people misunderstood about you as a testimony. What others saw as a flaw was the fingerprint of God on my destiny.

The gifts God placed inside of you are clues to your calling. Don't overlook them just because they come naturally. That's the evidence that they are God-breathed. You do not have to force what's divine. Hear me. There are gifts within you that have yet to be discovered. The unveiling will come as you walk by faith.

It's like peeling back the layers of an onion. Every layer you uncover brings you closer to the core of who you really are. However painful and humbling the process, it is always worth it. God hides greatness in layers. When you dare to go deep, you unlock dimensions of power, authority, and clarity that you didn't even know you carried.

But that wasn't the only turning point in my life.

Years later, I was a teenager on the verge of failure emotionally, academically, and spiritually. I was set to graduate high school with a 1.5 GPA. Although my self-worth was in shambles, I had decided I was going to sign up for beauty school.
On a Sunday afternoon, soon after I had made my decision, my pastor called for a prayer line. I don't even know why I got in line, I didn't expect anything. But when he reached me, he paused and said, "The Lord says go to college."

I was stunned.
College? I didn't feel smart enough.
College? I could barely write an essay.
College? I was the girl with the 1.5 GPA.
But then he said, "You're off limits until you get your degree. God has a plan for you."

That was the day something awakened in me. The power of God fell, and I wept hard. Not just because of the word, but because I realized God saw me. He believed in me before I could believe in myself.

That day, I began to walk differently. I started trusting the whispers of destiny again. And let me testify…

I didn't just go to college. I graduated with a 3.9 GPA, and I didn't stop there. I earned my master's degree, completed entrepreneurial school, and even became a Yale Fellow. God took the girl who barely made it out of high school and placed her in rooms she never dreamed of. Not because I was qualified. But because I was called.

He didn't stop with degrees. He gave me back my identity. He gave me a vision for my future. God showed me that my life had value, that I had a purpose, and that I was seen.

It's true what they say: "God qualifies those He calls." He peels back the layers, one by one, until you start to see the masterpiece He's been crafting all along.

There are layers you never knew existed. Some bring tears, and some reveal strengths you didn't know were buried. But every layer brings you closer to who God created you to be.

Every single step has been divinely orchestrated. I say to you, as someone who has walked through the fire and come out refined, God's plan for you is real. It is powerful. And it is bigger than your past.

"For I know the thoughts that I think toward you, saith the Lord, thoughts of peace, and not of evil, to give you an expected end."

—Jeremiah 29:11

This is not just a comforting verse. It is a divine decree. A strategic declaration from Heaven over your life. God's plan for you is one of prosperity, peace, and purpose. And every day, I rise with a single prayer on my lips: "Lord, reveal today's Kingdom assignment." Because when you live aligned with your Kingdom assignment, you step into a life of power, clarity, and overflow.

Friend, I share all of this because I know what it's like to feel unseen. To doubt your potential. To disqualify yourself because of your past. But I'm living proof that your beginning does not discredit your becoming. God already knew the end from the beginning, and He still chose you.

Don't ignore what came naturally to you as a child.
Don't underestimate the gifts that feel "too easy."
Don't abandon the calling just because it's buried under pain, failure, or fear. God is still peeling back the layers of your story. Trust me. What's at the core is beautiful.

So don't shrink back. Don't second guess your value. Don't wait until you feel "ready." You are already called. Already chosen. Already equipped.

The gifts in you are not random. They are required. The world needs what you carry. Heaven is waiting on your yes. So lean in, peel back the layers, seek God daily, and walk boldly into the destiny that's been waiting for you all along. God has a better future for you, one filled with fire, favor, and fulfillment. Now go forth and walk in it.

Discovering the Beauty in Unexpected Places

Friend, when life throws you a curveball, when the winds shift and you find yourself staring into the storm, do not be dismayed. The enemy wants you stuck in frustration, drowning in disappointment, and bound by despair. I came to stir your spirit to this truth: There is beauty even here. There are blessings hidden in what looks like brokenness. There is favor in what feels like failure. There is destiny unfolding in what the world calls a detour.

Every setback is a setup for revelation. Every trial is an invitation to transformation.

Hear me clearly: What if the challenge you're facing isn't a punishment but a passage? What if it's a divine invitation to shift your perspective and perceive the favor of God moving on your behalf? Don't just endure hardship. Extract the treasure buried beneath it.

Picture this. You are in the championship game of life. The scoreboard looks bleak. You are down by 15. The crowd is roaring, and your teammates are discouraged. Everything in the natural screams, "It's over," but something rises up in you. You silence the noise. You zoom out, and suddenly, you see it. The crowd cheering you on. The ones who've stood with you. The journey that brought you here. You remember the practices, the preparation, the purpose. You realize you are not defeated. You are being refined.

Instead of crumbling under pressure, you rise with Holy Spirit fire, fueled not by the score but by divine strength. That is what happens when you shift your perspective, when you stop looking at the battle and start seeing the breakthrough. When you stop counting the losses and start claiming the lessons. Step back. Look again. There is glory in the wilderness. There is water flowing in dry places.

"Behold, I will do a new thing; now it shall spring forth; shall ye not know it? I will even make a way in the wilderness, and rivers in the desert."

—Isaiah 43:19

This is not just a verse, it is a Heavenly command over your life. God is making a way right now, even when you can't see it. The wasteland of your pain is becoming the wellspring of your power. He is shifting the atmosphere, rerouting your path, and ushering in something entirely new.

So open your eyes. Open your spirit. Look again. There is purpose in the pressure. There is anointing in the adversity. There is beauty in the unexpected.

And you, child of God, are walking into it with boldness, grace, and unshakable faith. Let this be the day you stop asking, "Why me, Lord?" and start declaring, "Use me, Lord!" Because where the world sees ashes, you see oil. Where the world sees endings, you see new beginnings. You are aligned, assigned, and anointed for such a time as this.

My Testimony: Hidden Blessings in Hard Places

I've shared before that I had to overcome some tough seasons in my life. What I haven't fully shared is how deep that pain truly went. What happened next goes even deeper, into the battlefield of the mind, the fight for identity, and the war for destiny.

When I was just 14 or 15 years old, I was ready to end it all.

Yes, I had already made the decision. I was young, but the weight I carried was suffocating. I didn't fit in, no matter how hard I tried. The "friends" I had were fake, and the bullying I endured day in and day out left deep scars that no one could see. I was surrounded by noise, but drowning in silence. My mother was going through a divorce from the only father figure I had ever known, and my biological father made it clear: I was not his priority. I was walking wounded. I was rejected. I was abandoned. I was afraid.

I stopped showing up and stopped caring. I graduated high school with a 1.5 GPA, not because I lacked intelligence, but because I had stopped believing that my life had any value. I skipped classes to avoid the torment. I was the smallest girl in the room, with the shortest hair and the loudest pain. I had been bullied for years, and high school only amplified the cruelty. I was empty. Fragile. Lost.

And then came the day. The day I planned to end it all. I told myself no one would notice. No one would care. I had become a punching bag for others, but more tragically, for myself. The lies of the enemy were loud: "You're worthless. You're invisible. You're replaceable." But the devil is, and always will be, a liar. Right before I was about to give up, Heaven stepped in.

God interrupted the assignment of death with divine intervention. That day, He sent two weapons of deliverance: a song and a woman from my church who was like an aunt to me. At the exact moment I needed it most, she called. And that song? It was not just music. It was a prophetic sound. A divine dispatch. A war cry wrapped in a melody.

"Thou art my hiding place; thou shalt preserve me from trouble; thou shalt compass me about with songs of deliverance. Selah."

—Psalm 32:7

I did not just survive that day. I was delivered.

Fast forward to today, and let me speak this into the atmosphere: God has a plan for your life so powerful, so redemptive, so breathtaking, that if you could see the full picture, you'd never doubt Him again.

The same girl who once wanted to disappear is now living out a destiny she never imagined. Every single day, I wake up drenched in divine purpose. I walk in the miracles I prayed for, and in many I didn't even know I needed.

Those hidden blessings? They were always there. Waiting. Prepared in advance by a loving Father who was never absent, just working behind the scenes.

And let me tell you something, friend. He's doing the same for you. Look again. The very things sent to destroy you are the very things God will use to elevate you. The bullying? God used it. Remember how I said I was bullied for having short hair? At the time, it felt like humiliation, but God turned that into a platform. He gave me a vision to help other women embrace their beauty, and from that, I now empower other women through a thriving hair care line called Beautigrow. What once brought me shame is now blessing others. That's the God we serve.

"To appoint unto them that mourn in Zion, to give unto

them beauty for ashes, the oil of joy for mourning, the garment of praise for the spirit of heaviness."

—Isaiah 61:3

He doesn't just restore. He redeems. He multiplies. He weaponizes your wounds and turns them into wonders.

My friend, I speak this over your life:
It is time to come out of agreement with fear.
It is time to break the covenant with shame.
It is time to shake off the grave clothes of your past and step into the royal robes of your calling.

God is calling you to divine alignment. To fearless purpose. To unwavering obedience. Your pain has a purpose. Your past has a prophecy. Your obedience will unlock the overflow. So lift your eyes. Open your heart. And get ready to walk in the hidden blessings that have been waiting on your "yes."

This is not just your testimony.
This is your commissioning.
He's not finished with you yet.

Navigating the Unexpected Challenges of Doubt and Fear

Let me be clear from the start: I came to expose every lie, every fear, every internal thought that has been planted to stop your destiny. You see, discovering your divine purpose will not always feel like a gentle walk through the Garden of Eden. Often, it feels more like a battlefield where the war is not external but internal.

You will face doubt. You will hear the whispers of fear. You will wrestle with voices that question your worth, your ability, your qualifications. Hear me by the Spirit of God: those whispers are lies straight from the pit of hell. Their assignment is to silence you, to keep you stagnant, to delay what God has ordained.

Moses stood before a burning bush, trembling, questioning, afraid. But God did not entertain his excuses. God gave him a declaration: "I will be with thee." That is the only credential Moses needed. It is the only credential you need, too.

You must understand this: Satan does not need to attack your circumstances if he can sabotage your mindset. He is the father of lies, a deceiver so cunning that he will use your own voice against you. That is why your inner dialogue must come into divine alignment. When I caught myself thinking, "I'm not enough… I can't do this…" I had to rebuke it. Because God's Word says otherwise.

"I can do all things through Christ which strengtheneth me."

—Philippians 4:13

Not some things. Not the easy things. All things. You are divinely equipped to conquer the impossible because God is your source. If He is your strength, there is no excuse to live beneath your purpose.

There came a moment in my life when I had to make a decision not just to silence the lies, but to destroy them at the root. Listening to fear is one thing, but meditating on it gives it permission to multiply. So I stopped entertaining defeat. I stopped feeding my past. My past has nothing new to say to me. It cannot define my next chapter, and neither can yours.

Stop letting fear paralyze your movement. Stop letting doubt dictate your destiny. If you want to meet the person God created you to be, you have got to take giant leaps of faith.

Think of David, a teenage boy, overlooked by men but handpicked by God. When Goliath roared, David did not shrink. He stepped up. He refused Saul's armor because he trusted in God's strategy, not man's system. With one stone and unshakable faith, he took the giant down.

That same giant-killing potential is in you. It only emerges when you leap.

I will never forget the day my mother literally stepped into fire. When a neighbor's house burst into flames, she did not hesitate. She did not wait for a plan. She ran into that burning house and rescued a woman and her disabled son. In that moment, her potential met her purpose and fear had no place to stand. She took a giant leap of faith, much like Shadrach, Meshach, and Abednego stepping into the fiery furnace. Your bold obedience will open the door to your divine breakthrough. Let fear burn. Let doubt fall. Let purpose rise.

> **"Fear thou not; for I am with thee: be not dismayed; for I am thy God: I will strengthen thee; yea, I will help thee; yea, I will uphold thee with the right hand of my righteousness."**
>
> **—Isaiah 41:10**

So rise up, kingdom child of purpose. Your future is waiting, and you have been fortified for the fight.

Navigating by Faith: Rerouting from Setbacks and Divine Detours

Let us talk about the landmines that try to sabotage your journey: setbacks and detours.

Now, friend, setbacks are like giant hurdles that stand between us and our goals, threatening to knock us off course and derail our progress. Here is the thing: setbacks are not signs of failure. They are indicators of future power. They are divine disruptions meant to produce the perseverance needed for your next level.

When life hits hard and your plans seem shattered, do not collapse. Refocus. Regroup. Reignite your resolve. Dig deep, tap into your inner strength, and grow stronger and more resilient than ever before.

I have faced setbacks in business, in family, and in finances. What have I learned? Vision must remain unshaken. It is not about how long the journey takes; it is about refusing to stop until you arrive.

"My brethren, count it all joy when ye fall into divers temptations; knowing this, that the trying of your faith worketh patience. But let patience have her perfect work, that ye may be perfect and entire, wanting nothing."

—James 1:2-4

I have learned to fix my eyes on the vision, even in the storm. I remind myself: God finishes what He starts. Setbacks cannot cancel God's promises. If He started it in you, He will see it through. He which hath begun a good work in you will perform it until the day of Jesus Christ.

So when life throws its worst, you declare God's best. You keep walking. You keep building. You keep birthing.

Again, it is not about how long the journey takes. It is about refusing to stop until you arrive. Setbacks are not the end of the road. They are the beginning of a new chapter filled with growth, resilience, and strength.

Detours

My friend, hear me today. Life's journey is not a straight path. You will face setbacks. You will encounter delays. And yes, there will be detours. Hear this: detours are not denials. They are divine disruptions, orchestrated by the hand of God to reroute you, reposition you, and realign you with your destiny.

That detour is not designed to destroy your progress. It is designed to develop your purpose. When you are driving down a familiar road and suddenly see a detour sign, frustration rises. But I declare to you today: what seems like a delay is actually divine redirection. You are not being pushed off course. You are being pushed into promise.

You see, detours expose you to places you never would have gone on your own. They take you through neighborhoods you have never explored, territories that hold hidden treasures, new revelation, new relationships, new resources, new realms.

Do not curse the detour. Celebrate it. It is your training ground. Your proving ground. Your preparation for promotion.

God is the Master Strategist. He is not intimidated by your detour, nor is He surprised by your delay.

"A man's heart deviseth his way: but the Lord directeth his steps."

—Proverbs 16:9

Oh, glory to God, He is directing your steps even now. When you cannot trace His hand, trust His plan, because the God who called you is faithful to complete what He started in you.

David understood this. Psalm 23 tells us that even though he walked through the valley of the shadow of death, he feared no evil. Why? Because God was with him. David faced enemies, betrayal, and obstacles, but he kept moving. He did not die in the valley. He came through with victory, with testimony, with anointing. And you will too.

I speak over you today: your detour is setting you up for a greater destination. What looked like a delay is actually acceleration in disguise. What felt like rejection is redirection. What seemed like the end is the setup for your next beginning.

You are not alone. The hand of God is upon you. The Spirit of the Lord is going before you. Angels are clearing the way. Every setback is a setup. Every detour is destiny disguised.

So rise up in faith. Shake off disappointment. Speak to your future with boldness. Declare the Word of the Lord. Walk with confidence, knowing that your steps are ordered, your path is blessed, and your destiny is unstoppable.

This is your time. This is your turn. This detour will lead you straight into destiny. Amen, and so it is.

Finding Joy and Fulfillment While Living Out Your Purpose

Friend, as we press forward in our pursuit of purpose, let us not overlook this truth: the process is just as powerful as the promise. Every step, every struggle, every season is significant. You are not simply on your way to purpose; you are walking in purpose with every faithful stride.

The obstacles you've overcome, the lessons you've absorbed, the tears you've cried, have all brought you closer to the divine destiny that God designed for you before the foundation of the world. In the middle of it all, yes, even in the pain, there is joy and fulfillment. A holy satisfaction that this world cannot give and cannot take away.

I declare to you today: nothing in your life has been wasted. The heartbreaks, the closed doors, the delays, the betrayals, the battles, God has used it all for His glory and your good. What looked like rejection was divine redirection. What felt like the end was really God preparing a new beginning. Amen!

Let me share this with you. At first, I couldn't see it. I was fixated on the doors that had slammed shut; blinded by fear; paralyzed by disappointment; tormented by anger, jealousy, and unforgiveness. The moment I released it all, the bitterness, the resentment, the comparison, the pain of the past, that was the moment I saw the open door in front of me. God had been holding it open all along, waiting for me to walk through.

Let me be transparent with you. I've walked through the shadows.

God had purpose even when I tried to end my life. He was present through the pain of miscarriage. He was working during academic failures, the breaking point in my marriage, the agony of family dysfunction. He had a plan when friends turned their backs, when racial injustice struck deep, and when I nearly died giving birth. He was sovereign when loved ones were snatched from my life unexpectedly. Yes, He had a purpose in it all. What the enemy meant for evil, God is using for good.

"And we know that all things work together for good to them that love God, to them who are the called according to his purpose."

—Romans 8:28

That is not just a verse; that's a war cry. A reminder that God is weaving every thread of your story into a tapestry of glory.

Now hear this: You are God's masterpiece. You are not random. You are not forgotten. You are not a mistake.

"For we are his workmanship, created in Christ Jesus unto good works, which God hath before ordained that we should walk in them."

—Ephesians 2:10

You have been created on purpose for a purpose. And not only that, God has already made provision for the vision. What He prepared in advance means the breakthrough has already been set in motion. The doors are already open. The path is waiting for your feet.

So now, it's time to step into it. Boldly. Unapologetically. Unshakably. Hebrews tells us to come boldly to the throne of grace, and I say to you, come with confidence. You are anointed for this. Appointed for this. Equipped for this.

As you close this chapter and open a new one, you're not just discovering treasure; you're becoming the treasure. There is gold in you. Glory in you. Power in you. Purpose buried deep within you; and now is the time to unearth it. You are shifting. Evolving. Growing. With each shift, God is revealing more. So rise up. Shake off the old. Step into the new. You are walking into a season of joy, fulfillment, and unshakable clarity of purpose. God has gone before you. Now go and live out your divine assignment with holy fire and fearless determination.

AIM Shift (*Always In Motion to Shift*)

Each chapter of your journey comes with an AIM Shift, because to AIM is to be Always In Motion. You cannot grow without movement. You cannot evolve without shifting. These AIM Shifts are your divine action steps, tools to transform your thinking, recalibrate your perspective, and unlock your next level.

AIM Shift 1: Reflect Deeply on Your Life to Unlock Your Purpose

Before you can walk fully in your purpose, you must first understand what drives you.

Purpose is not something you stumble upon; it is something you uncover, something you unearth from within. It is already inside you, buried beneath fear, disappointment, and the noise of life. Today, I declare: the excavation begins.

This is your AIM Shift, your divine invitation to pause, reflect, and realign. You are Always In Motion, but movement without meaning leads to misdirection. So let's make this motion intentional.

Step 1: Identify Your Core Values

Your core values are the foundation stones of your destiny. These are the convictions etched into your spirit by the hand of God Himself. They guide how you think, how you love, how you lead, and how you live. What are the things you hold closest to your heart? For some, it might be faith, love, service, or growth. These values are the bedrock of your purpose. Ask yourself: "What do I want to stand for?" Not what the world says you should be or what others expect. But who did God create you to be at your core?

Start here. Write them down. Speak them aloud. Let Heaven hear you declare them.

Examples of Core Values

- *Faith*
- *Integrity*
- *Creativity*
- *Service*
- *Leadership*
- *Freedom*
- *Joy*
- *Excellence*
- *Resilience*
- *Love*
- *Growth*
- *Peace*

Let the Holy Spirit guide you as you journal and meditate on these: Choose three to five values that burn in your heart. These are your spiritual anchors, your compass in the chaos.

Reflective Questions to Uncover Your Core Values

1. *When do I feel most like myself?* Think of moments when you felt the most alive, at peace, or full of purpose. What values were you honoring?

2. *What qualities do I admire in others?* The greatness you recognize in others often mirrors what God has deposited in you. The people you look up to can reflect the traits and values you cherish, like honesty, resilience, kindness, or boldness.

3. *What makes me angry, sad, or frustrated?* What injustice makes your spirit rise up? What pain do you feel called to heal? Sometimes, your anger reveals your assignment.

4. *What am I most proud of in my life?* Think about meaningful achievements or moments. Look at the victories, not just the visible ones, but the internal ones too. The times you chose to rise instead of retreat. What values were present? (e.g., perseverance, creativity, faith)

5. *What do I want to be remembered for?* Imagine someone giving a eulogy or writing your legacy. What values do you want them to say you stood for? What legacy do you want to leave behind?

6. *In difficult decisions, what principle do I refuse to compromise on?* This could be integrity, loyalty, honesty, or compassion, whatever anchors you when life gets tough.

7. *What brings me joy and deep fulfillment?* Purpose and joy are married. Joy is a clue to your values. Is it helping others, solving problems, creating beauty, or leading change?

8. *What do I consistently spend time, energy, or money on?* Your behavior often reflects your real values. Look at your calendar and bank account; they tell a story.

My friend, this is not a surface-level exercise. This is deep work. As you take time to reflect, I believe God is whispering to you, pointing out the core of who you really are, and who He's calling you to become.

Do not rush this moment. Do not minimize this reflection. Because in this shift, you are not just identifying values; you are reclaiming your identity, your clarity, your voice, and your vision. Your values reveal your calling. Your calling ignites your purpose. Let this AIM Shift be the divine recalibration that launches you into your next dimension.

Choose three to five values that burn in your heart. These are your spiritual anchors, your compass in the chaos.

Now, write. Reflect. Release.
Prepare for what God is about to unlock in you.

Step 2: Write Your Core Purpose Statement

Your Core Purpose Statement is more than just a sentence. It is a prophetic declaration. A divine compass. A clarion call that anchors you to your assignment and reveals who you are at your essence, not just what you do.

It transcends your titles and rises above your roles. You are not defined by what you do, but by who you are. Roles may shift, mother, entrepreneur, educator, leader, artist, but your core identity remains unshaken. You are not your job. You are not your circumstances. You are the intentional handiwork of the Creator, designed for impact, influence, and legacy. This statement is your inner truth revealed, the sacred expression of how God wired you, why you were born, and who you're called to serve.

My Example Core Purpose Statement

"I am an empathetic, prolific visionary and an innovative steward dedicated to nurturing the soul and serving others."

This is who I am, no matter the season, no matter the setting. Whether I'm parenting, building businesses, or mentoring others, this truth governs my choices and grounds my identity.

Let me break it down:

Empathetic – I feel deeply. I understand. I connect with compassion.

Prolific visionary – I see beyond. I create. I dream. I architect futures.

Innovative steward – I manage well. I adapt. I lead with dynamic excellence and intention.

Dedicated to nurturing the soul and serving others – My mission is clear. I help others grow in purpose and value. My impact is eternal.

Now, it's your turn to declare who you are. Take the values you uncovered and craft your Core Purpose Statement. This is your personal creed. Your identity blueprint.

Use the simple yet powerful formula below:

Core Purpose Statement Template

"I am a(n) [**core trait**], [**strength/skill**], and [**unique role**] dedicated to [**mission**] and [**who/what you serve**]."

Examples for Inspiration

- *"I am a resilient encourager, creative communicator, and purpose-driven mentor dedicated to uplifting hearts and empowering people to walk in their calling."*

- *"I am an empathetic listener, problem-solver, and passionate advocate dedicated to guiding individuals through life's transitions and helping them discover their true potential."*

- *"I am a determined visionary, strategic thinker, and innovative leader dedicated to driving positive change and empowering communities to thrive."*

- *"I am an innovative designer, detail-oriented thinker, and purposeful creator dedicated to crafting meaningful experiences that connect people and enhance lives."*

- *"I am a compassionate listener, nurturing coach, and growth-oriented mentor dedicated to helping individuals heal and transform their lives through personalized guidance."*

This is more than an exercise, it's a divine unveiling. As you write your statement, do not rush. Ask the Holy Spirit to reveal the language of your destiny. Let God inform your identity. This statement will become your filter for decisions and the fire behind your focus. So now, my friend, write it. Speak it. Own it. Live it. Let the world experience the radiant glory of who you truly are.

Step 3: Create Your Purpose Buckets

Now that you've identified your core values and written your Core Purpose Statement, it's time to bring structure to your vision. You are stepping into strategic alignment. This next phase will help you categorize your life by divine intention.

We call this system: *8 Purpose Buckets*. To break them down, we will use this formula:

Formula: (LSP Goals + SSP Goals = 8 Purpose Buckets)

What Are Purpose Buckets?

Purpose Buckets are life categories that carry the weight of your calling. They are the areas where your values show up and where your purpose is lived out daily, consistently, and intentionally. Think of them as containers that hold your dreams, goals, and assignments. These buckets keep your focus sharp, your goals organized, and your life aligned with Heaven's design for you.

Ask yourself, "Where in my life do I want to live out my purpose most consistently?" Let that question guide how you build your buckets. These are not just categories, they are spiritual mandates.

Two Pillars of Purpose Buckets

You'll divide your life into two pillars:

LSP Goals – Long Success Purpose Goals (Three Buckets)
SSP Goals – Short Success Purpose Goals (Five Buckets)

Together, they form your *8 Purpose Buckets:* Your personal blueprint for building a life of impact, fulfillment, and divine order.

LSP Goals: Long Success Purpose Goals (3 Buckets)

These are your foundational life goals. They do not change because they reflect the core of who you are becoming. These long-term objectives sustain your growth and form the backbone of your overall vision.

We call these your **M, M, & M:**

- *Major Goals* (Life Goals)

- *Mindset Goals* (Development Goals)

- *Miscellaneous Goals* (Personal or Creative Goals)

Write these three categories down. They are fixed. They serve as your spiritual scaffolding, the structure that supports all future growth.

SSP Goals: Short Success Purpose Goals (5 Buckets)

These are short-term, actionable goals that align with your bigger picture. They are your current assignments, the areas God is calling you to steward in this season. These goals are designed to be precise, accountable, and season-bound, helping you build momentum while staying rooted in your purpose.

Here Are Examples of SSP Goal Buckets (Customize as Needed):
- *Family and Relationships*

- *Work and Professional Life*
- *Education and Personal Growth*
- *Church and Community Engagement*
- *Business and Entrepreneurship*
- *Health and Wellness*
- *Finance and Wealth Building*
- *Friendships and Mentorship*
- *Creative Expression*
- *Social or Global Impact*

Example Layout: My 8 Purpose Buckets

LSP Goals (Long-Term):

1. Major
2. Mindset
3. Miscellaneous

SSP Goals (Short-Term):

4. Family and Relationships
5. Career or Professional Goals
6. Personal Growth or Education
7. Church or Community Engagement
8. Business or Entrepreneurship

Why This Matters:

Your LSP Goals act as your foundation. Your SSP Goals are your current assignments. Together, they create a balanced and purpose-driven life that is intentional, sustainable, and impactful. This structure becomes your personal roadmap, a living strategy that ensures every move you make, every goal you set, and every dream you chase aligns with your God-given destiny. So now, my friend, organize, align, and advance. You're not just setting goals. You're stewarding your purpose.

Step 4: Fill Your Buckets with Purpose Goals

Now is the time to step boldly into action. You've clarified your Core Values, written your Core Purpose Statement, and created your 8 Purpose Buckets. Now, let's fill those buckets with intentional, purpose-driven goals that reflect the assignment on your life. This is where vision meets strategy and where you move from revelation to manifestation.

What Are Purpose Goals?

Purpose goals are not about daily to-do lists or random resolutions. They are the divinely inspired objectives that align with your values, ignite your passion, and move you toward destiny. They are the "why" behind every decision, the deeper reason you rise each morning. These goals are value-aligned and Spirit-led. They point to the legacy you are called to leave.

"And the Lord answered me, and said, Write the vision, and make it plain upon tables, that he may run that readeth it."

—Habakkuk 2:2

Why Purpose Goals Matter

We make countless decisions daily, but what drives them? When you know why, your decisions become clearer. No more wandering or second-guessing. Your goals become a compass, guiding your time, your energy, and your focus. So, my friend, ask yourself: What is God calling me to build with my life? What legacy do I want to leave? What truly brings me peace, fulfillment, and joy? Let these questions lead you to the kind of clarity that anchors your soul.

How to Discover Your Purpose Goals

Now, how do we discover these essential goals, the ones that truly matter?

- How do we tap into the heart of what God has placed inside us? Take a deep breath, friend, and let's dive into it together. Here are a few questions to help guide you: What do I really want to achieve in life? This is the big question. Take a moment to dream.

- What are the things you really want to accomplish, not just in the next year, but in the big picture? These are the dreams that God has placed on your heart. It could be something as grand as changing the world or as personal as creating a loving home for your family.

- What Does My "End Goal" Look Like? Think about your life years from now. When you look back, what do you want to see? That is your end result. Whether it's raising a family with love, running a successful business, or becoming a person of deep spiritual wisdom, your end goal is the culmination of your efforts. Focus on that, and let it guide your actions.

- What Does Success Mean to Me? Success does not look the same for everyone. For you, it might mean peace, freedom, or joy. It could be financial independence, personal growth, or making an impact. Whatever it is, define it clearly for yourself. When you know what success looks like, you can set your course toward it.

- What Brings Me Joy and Peace? What gives you a deep sense of fulfillment and peace? This is often a clue to what's most important. If you find joy in helping others, then your goals may revolve around service. If your heart is full when you're creating something, that could point to your purpose goals.

Pay attention to these moments. They'll show you where you should focus your energy.

Steps to Help You Write Your Purpose Goals

- *Be Specific:* The more specific you are, the clearer your path becomes. Don't just say, "I want to be happy." Say, "I want to feel peace and fulfillment in my work and relationships." This helps you know exactly what you're aiming for.

- *Use Positive Language:* Focus on what you want to achieve, rather than what you want to avoid. Instead of saying, "I don't want to be stressed," say, "I want to lead a calm and balanced life."

- *Review and Adjust:* Your goals will evolve, and that's okay. Regularly check in with yourself. Do they still align with where God is taking you? Adjust and refine them as necessary. Life is a journey.

Now, Let's Fill Your 8 Purpose Buckets
List 3-5 purpose-aligned goals under each category.
Here are examples to inspire you:

LSP GOALS (Long-Term, Foundational)

1. **Major Goals:** (Your legacy. Your life's big assignments.)
   - Achieve financial freedom and fund global missions
   - Establish a family foundation that empowers underserved youth
   - Write a book that transforms lives and outlives you
2. **Mindset Goals:** strengthen your inner world. Elevate your thinking.

- Cultivate a faith-filled, abundance mindset through daily declarations

- Break generational patterns by embracing emotional healing

- Read one growth book a month to fuel spiritual and mental renewal

3. **Miscellaneous Goals:** Personal, creative, or joyful pursuits that enrich your life.

- Learn a new language or instrument

- Travel to one new nation each year

- Start a podcast or blog to share your voice with the world

SSP GOALS (Short-Term, Actionable)

4. **Family Goals:** build intentional love and lasting legacy.

- Have weekly one-on-one time with each child

- Start monthly family devotionals

- Host an annual family vision retreat

5. **Church / Faith / Community:** Deepen your walk with God and impact your community.

- Serve consistently in your church ministry or small group

- Lead a prayer call or Bible study once a month

- Volunteer monthly at a local shelter or outreach program

6. **Business / Entrepreneurship:** Advance in the marketplace with purpose and integrity.

- Grow your business by 25% over the next 12 months

- Launch a purpose-driven product or service by Q4

- Mentor one emerging entrepreneur this year

7. **Career / Work Goals:** Climb, lead, or pivot with purpose.

- Position yourself for promotion by mastering a new skill
- Create boundaries to preserve peace and balance
- Get certified in a new area that aligns with your calling

8. **Education / Personal Growth:** Lifelong learning fuels destiny.

- Complete a professional certification in the next six months
- Join a mastermind group or mentorship program
- Read a new book every month to expand perspective and vision

Putting It All Into Action

Now that your goals are written, it's time to activate them. Ask yourself daily: "Does this decision move me closer to my purpose or further from it?" Use your Purpose Buckets as a filter. Let them guide how you spend your time, energy, and resources.

Writing your purpose goals is not just a productivity strategy, it is a prophetic act. When you put vision on paper, you give it permission to manifest. When you commit your goals to God, you invite Heaven into your planning.

So go ahead, write boldly, plan prayerfully, and execute relentlessly. You are not just chasing goals. You are building a life of meaning, legacy, and divine impact.

"Commit thy works unto the Lord, and thy thoughts shall be established."

—Proverbs 16:3

CHAPTER 2: FROM CONFUSION TO CLARITY: 12 KEYS TO EMBRACING YOUR GOD-GIVEN PURPOSE

"Give a big hug to your purpose."

—*Shaasia Nance*

Congratulations, friend! You've taken the first step on this incredible journey of self-discovery. But what does that really mean? In this chapter, we are going to explore the importance of wholeheartedly embracing your purpose.

Have you ever felt like you're just drifting through life, unsure of your direction or purpose? I've been there too. Here is what I learned while I was drifting, instead of taking the right steps to embrace and pursue my purpose. I found myself stuck in a repetitive cycle, doing the same things day after day, yet expecting different results. Looking back, I realize how foolish it was to think that repetition would somehow bring change. I had to make a choice to take new steps to embrace God's plans for my life.

As we learned in the last chapter, God has a specific purpose for each of us. Too many of us have spent years searching for purpose outside of ourselves when the answers were always within. God has uniquely designed each of us with a purpose in mind, and He's equipped us with everything we need to fulfill it. However, in order to see the full effect of our purpose, we must embrace it.

Now, let's dive into how we can align our hearts with God's beautiful plan by embracing twelve essential keys that will help us grasp our purpose, just like the woman with the issue of blood. She reached out and touched the hem of Jesus' garment, seizing her opportunity for healing. In doing so, she not only found physical healing but was also given a brand-new perspective and purpose in life.

To "embrace" means to hold closely, accept, and support. These twelve keys are the things we must accept and support if we want to see real change in our lives. Only then can we fully experience all the amazing things God has placed in our hearts.

Key Number 1: Embrace Seeking Guidance, Turning to God for Direction and Wisdom

As you navigate the journey of embracing your purpose, it is important to remember that you do not have to do it alone. In fact, God has promised to guide you every step of the way, providing you with the wisdom and direction you need to fulfill His purpose for your life.

Think about it like this: when you're lost in unfamiliar territory, what's the first thing you do? You pull out a map or GPS and turn to someone who knows the way. Your GPS is the Holy Spirit. He is the guide who sees the whole path. He knows the way and will guide you with His wisdom and direction.

"Trust in the Lord with all thine heart; and lean not unto thine own understanding. In all thy ways acknowledge him, and he shall direct thy paths."

—Proverbs 3:5–6

God has all the wisdom, and He has given us that wisdom through the Holy Spirit. We need the Holy Spirit's intelligence to embrace our purpose.

Key Number 2: Embrace Surrender, Surrender Is Not Defeat, It Is Dominion

Surrender is not a weakness. Surrender is a strategy. When you surrender to God, you are not giving up, you are giving over your plans, your time, and your understanding to the One who authored your destiny before the foundation of the earth.

Let me tell you something, my friend: surrender is the highest form of spiritual intelligence. It is the moment you stop struggling and start aligning. It is where your will bows, and His will breaks through.

I used to say, "I don't have time," but the Holy Spirit intercepted me and said, "No, you don't have vision." I was managing hours instead of stewarding purpose. I was counting minutes instead of multiplying moments. God spoke clearly: "I am not asking you to manage time. I AM time." That revelation shattered my excuses. He showed me I did not have twenty-four hours to waste, but 86,400 seconds every day to invest into eternity.

I made a lot of excuses, blaming it on my job or claiming there wasn't enough time in the day. One day, as I sought God, He told me I had no excuse not to pursue the things He placed inside me. I argued, "But God, there's no time," and He responded, "Let ME change your perspective on time."

As I listened to the Spirit, I realized I couldn't manage time because God is time. I couldn't change the number of hours in a day, twenty-four hours are a given, but I could change how I spent them. I had been neglecting divine potential by watching others live out their purpose, while mine was still on the shelf. When I surrendered my time, my habits, and my distractions, I stepped into a new realm of clarity, power, and productivity.

I stopped watching and started warring. I stopped scrolling and started building. I stopped consuming and started creating. The moment I surrendered control, God released acceleration.

Listen to me: God does not anoint chaos. He anoints order. And order begins with surrender. You cannot activate divine strategy with a carnal mindset. You must come out of survival mode and step into kingdom flow. There is a difference between busyness and fruitfulness, and the bridge between the two is intentional surrender.

"Delight thyself also in the Lord; and he shall give thee the desires of thine heart. Commit thy way unto the Lord; trust also in him; and he shall bring it to pass."

—Psalm 37:4–5

When you delight in the Lord, He begins to recenter your desires. Your goals shift. Your time multiplies. Your dreams become downloads from heaven. Your excuses are deconstructed by divine wisdom. This is your moment.

I declare over you today:

You will not waste another second. You will not bow to procrastination. You will not surrender to fear.
You are stepping into a new season of discipline, divine focus, and supernatural acceleration.
You are reclaiming your time, your purpose, and your destiny.

Lift your hands and declare it:

"I surrender not to quit, but to conquer! I release my plans to receive God's perfect will. I align with divine timing. I will steward my seconds, maximize my moments, and walk fully in my kingdom assignment. In Jesus' name, amen!"

Key Number 3: Embracing Patience, The Power in the Waiting Room of Destiny

Ah, patience. That divine fruit of the Spirit we love to quote but struggle to cultivate. In a world that celebrates instant results and microwave success, patience becomes your superpower. You see, patience is not passivity. It is prophetic positioning. It is not sitting still. It is standing firm. It is not losing time. It is gaining alignment.

Patience is the womb of destiny. It is where God hides the masterpiece until the unveiling is complete. If you want the fullness of what God has for you, you must learn how to wait without wavering.

Let me paint the picture for you. Have you ever been at the airport, waiting on a delayed flight? Frustration creeps in. You start checking the time. You pace. You sigh. What if, instead of focusing on the delay, you focused on the destination?

What if you shifted your perspective and declared,

"This delay is divine. God is preparing the runway for something greater than I imagined."

Let me tell you something I learned by revelation. Sometimes, we think we are waiting on God, but God is waiting on us. He was waiting on me to mature. Waiting on me to get in position. Waiting on me to take authority and walk in the power He already placed within me. When I stopped struggling and started aligning, everything began to shift. I began to meditate on the Word that says patience produces perfect work, making you whole, complete, and lacking nothing.

"But let patience have her perfect work, that ye may be perfect and entire, wanting nothing."

—James 1:4

> *"He hath made every thing beautiful in his time: also he hath set the world in their heart, so that no man can find out the work that God maketh from the beginning to the end."*

—Ecclesiastes 3:11

These words carry power. Everything becomes beautiful in its time. That includes you. Your dreams. Your purpose. Your assignment. Your relationships. Your healing. Your breakthrough. It is all on Heaven's clock, not yours.

So I decree over you today:

You will not abort the process. You will not despise the delay. You will wait well, war wisely, and walk boldly. You will hold your peace and let patience perfect you. Every delay is divine. Every waiting room is a workshop. Every setback is a setup for glory.

Lift your voice and declare:

"I trust God's timing. I will not rush the process. I will not fear the wait. I am being perfected. I am being positioned. When my time comes, I will be ready. In Jesus' name, amen."

Key Number 4: Embracing Hearing God's Whispers, Tuning Into the Frequency of Heaven

God has already planted the seeds of our calling within us, and He's just waiting for us to listen and respond.

Before the earth was set on its axis, God encoded your calling into Heaven's map of your very being. The seeds of your purpose were planted in eternity.

Now, God is whispering, calling you to awaken and activate what He's already placed inside of you. God is always speaking, my friend. The question is, are you positioned to hear?

In a world full of noise, opinions, notifications, and distractions, hearing the still, small voice of God requires intentional alignment. It is not about volume. It is about frequency. Heaven has a frequency, and those who walk in purpose learn how to tune their spirits to it.

Think about this.

Have you ever been in a noisy room, and someone says your name? Despite the chaos, you instantly recognize it. That is because your name carries a unique resonance with your identity. Likewise, God is calling your name. He's whispering your assignment. He's speaking direction, strategy, and divine revelation.

Here is the truth. You cannot hear God clearly when you are tuned into everything else. You have to silence the noise of the culture, cancel the static of doubt, and shut down the background music of fear. You have to create sacred space and a listening posture to hear the whisper of the Holy Spirit.

"And thine ears shall hear a word behind thee, saying, This is the way, walk ye in it, when ye turn to the right hand, and when ye turn to the left."

—Isaiah 30:21

God is speaking, even in your confusion, even in your indecision. His voice is behind you, guiding you with clarity and power.

So I decree over you today:

Your ears are open to the frequency of the Spirit. Your heart is aligned with Heaven's sound. You will not follow a stranger's voice. You will hear the voice of the Shepherd and follow without fear.

Lift your voice and declare:

"I hear the whispers of God. I walk in divine direction. I am led by the Spirit. I am tuned in, turned on, and fully activated to respond to Heaven's call. I hear, I obey, and I advance."

Key Number 5: Embracing Perseverance, Standing Tall in the Fire and Pressing Forward with Power

Let me tell you this. Perseverance is the secret weapon of champions. It is the refusal to quit. It is the decision to keep going even when everything around you says stop. It is a spiritual force, an unyielding courage that aligns your will with Heaven's agenda and refuses to let go until breakthrough comes.

When you are walking in divine purpose, challenges are not optional. They are inevitable. But listen carefully. Opposition is often confirmation. If Hell is coming against you, it is because Heaven has already spoken for you. You are not just enduring. You are advancing.

Picture this. You are climbing a steep, rocky mountain. Your legs are trembling. The terrain is brutal. The air is thin. Yet, you press on. One step after the next. Why? Because there is glory at the peak. Destiny is calling, and giving up is not an option.

You do not need ease. You need endurance. You do not need comfort. You need conviction. You do not need escape. You need empowerment. Let this truth settle in your spirit. Every step you take in faith is declaring to the enemy, "I will not break. I will not bend. I will not bow. I will finish my race with fire."

"Blessed is the man that endureth temptation: for when he is tried, he shall receive the crown of life, which the Lord hath promised to them that love him."

—James 1:12

This is not just a test. It is a setup for your reward. Perseverance produces legacy. It opens doors to realms of blessing reserved for the unwavering.

So right now, I decree over you:

You will not faint. You will not fall. You are strong in the Lord and in the power of His might. Every setback is becoming a setup. Every delay is working for your destiny. Every trial is birthing triumph.

Speak this over your life:

"I am built for this. I press toward the mark. I stand when others fall. I endure through adversity. I am crowned with life. I am a finisher. In Jesus' name, I will not quit. I will conquer."

Key Number 6: Embracing Faith, Believing in God's Promises

To embrace God's beautiful plan, we must cultivate faith. It is about believing in God's promises, even when circumstances seem bleak. Faith is like a seed. It may start small, but with nurturing, it grows into something strong.

Faith is the foundation of our relationship with God. Let us water the seeds of faith within our hearts, trusting that His plan is unfolding, even when we cannot yet see the results.

Faith is the currency of the Kingdom. It is the invisible force that gives substance to your future and anchors your destiny in the promises of God. Without it, you cannot move mountains. Without it, you cannot access the supernatural. And without it, you cannot fully walk in the authority you were born to carry.

To embrace God's divine plan, you must speak what you see in the spirit until you see what you spoke in the natural. Faith declares the end from the beginning and keeps pressing forward, even when nothing looks like it is working.

Faith is not wishful thinking. It is the unwavering belief that if God said it, it is already done, sealed in eternity and waiting for your agreement to manifest in time.

Even when you are walking through a storm.
Even when you are staring at lack.
Even when the doctor's report says otherwise. Your faith says, "Nevertheless, I believe God."

> **"Now faith is the substance of things hoped for, the evidence of things not seen."**
>
> *—Hebrews 11:1*

Let me speak to your spirit:

You are not bound by what you see. You are anchored in what God said. You are not shaken by the facts. You are stabilized by the truth. You are not waiting for confirmation. You are moving with conviction. Faith is your war cry. Faith is your weapon. Faith is your access pass into realms unseen.

So today, rise up in boldness. Nurture the seed of faith within you. Speak life over your purpose. Declare the Word over your situation. Prophesy to your future.

Say it out loud:

"I walk by faith and not by sight. I believe God's Word above all else. I will see what He promised. I will possess what He declared. I am moving from faith to faith, from glory to glory, from promise to possession!"

Now is not the time to shrink back. It is the time to stand firm, trust radically, and believe fiercely.

Key Number 7: Embracing Growth, Stepping Out of Comfort Zones

Growth is not optional; it is essential. To live in alignment with God's purpose, you must refuse to settle in comfort and step boldly into the unfamiliar. God did not anoint you to survive. He anointed you to expand, to evolve, and to dominate in every sphere of influence to which He has called you.

Like a muscle, growth demands resistance. It will stretch you. It will test you. But it will also strengthen you. When God is calling you higher, you cannot afford to remain where it is easy. He is stretching your capacity, deepening your roots, and preparing you for greater influence, greater authority, and greater manifestation.

Just like a tree must send its roots deep to stand tall, you must allow God to stretch you emotionally, spiritually, and mentally so you can stand firm in your calling. Comfort zones are graveyards for destiny. Growth zones are birthplaces for miracles. Your comfort zone may feel safe, but it can be the very place where dreams die. True growth is often birthed in discomfort, where miracles begin.

"I can do all things through Christ which strengtheneth me."

—Philippians 4:13

This is not the time to shrink. It is the time to expand.
This is not the time to play small. It is the time to take territory.

This is your moment to grow through what you go through.

Speak this over your life right now, with power and boldness:

"I can do all things through Jesus Christ who gives me strength! I will not shrink back. I will not play small. I am being stretched, strengthened, and set apart for greatness. I embrace growth in every area of my life, in Jesus' name!"

Key Number 8: Embracing God's Blessings, Stepping into the Overflow of Abundant Life

You were not created to live in lack, limitation, or spiritual poverty. You were designed, by divine intent, to live in the overflow of God's goodness, drenched in the abundance of His blessings, walking in the fullness of your purpose with power and clarity.

When you align with Heaven's plan, abundance becomes your portion. You do not have to chase blessings. They will chase you down. Why? Because the Kingdom within you is bursting with treasure. The greatest blessing God has ever given you is not material; it is you. You are the treasure. You are the vessel. You are the carrier of divine inheritance.

You were worth the blood of Jesus. You were worth the cross. So, stop looking around for what is already inside. The power, the provision, the promise, it is already in you. God placed greatness inside of you. It is time to open the treasure chest of your soul and let the riches of purpose, wisdom, creativity, and divine potential overflow.

> *"The thief cometh not, but for to steal, and to kill, and to destroy: I am come that they might have life, and that they might have it more abundantly."*
>
> *—John 10:10*

Let this verse shatter the spirit of scarcity off your life. You were not born to survive. You were born to thrive. You were not saved to settle. You were redeemed to reign.

Right now, declare this over yourself with prophetic boldness:

"I am the blessed of the Lord. I walk in abundance. I overflow with favor, with purpose, with divine resources. The Kingdom within me lacks nothing!"

God has placed a river of blessing inside of you. Now, it is time to unblock the flow, release the treasure, and live in the divine overflow. You are not waiting on the blessing. You are the blessing. A lot of times, we focus on outward blessings and forget to explore the beautiful inner blessings God has placed inside us. Open the treasure chest and discover the abundance of wealth that will pour out of you.

Key Number 9: Embracing Gratitude, Activating the Supernatural Through Thanksgiving

Gratitude is not just a good habit. It is a spiritual weapon.

It shifts atmospheres. It disarms the enemy. It realigns your heart with Heaven. When you live with a grateful spirit, you position yourself to receive more, to see more clearly, and to walk in joy that defies circumstances.

In a world obsessed with hustle, comparison, and what is next, gratitude anchors you in God's presence. It reminds your soul that you already have access to divine peace, provision, and power. Whether in seasons of overflow or in the valley of waiting, gratitude teaches you to praise God not just for what He has done, but for who He is.

Think about it: when you stop and take inventory of the blessings around you, your breath, your purpose, your growth, you begin to see through the lens of Heaven. What once looked like obstacles now looks like opportunities. What once felt like pressure now feels like preparation. Gratitude turns your "Why me?" into "Thank You, Lord." It shifts your focus from what is missing to what is multiplying.

> *"Praise ye the Lord. O give thanks unto the Lord; for he is good: for his mercy endureth for ever."*
>
> —*Psalm 106:1*

Let this be your decree:

"I live in perpetual thanksgiving. I see God in every detail. I recognize miracles in motion. I give thanks in all things, and because of this, I will never lack."

Gratitude is not weakness. It is wisdom. It is one of the most powerful postures you can take on your journey to purpose. When you cultivate a heart of thankfulness, you begin to move in sync with the rhythm of Heaven.

So today, open your mouth and give God thanks. Thank Him for what was, what is, and what is to come. Thank Him for the seen and the unseen, the open doors and the ones He lovingly closed. Because when you walk in gratitude, you walk in victory.

Key Number 10: Embracing an Abundance Mindset, Living from the Overflow

You were never meant to live with a scarcity mentality. Lack is not your portion. Limitation is not your identity. You serve a God of overflow, El Shaddai, the God of more than enough. To fully step into the abundant life Jesus promised, you must first shift your mindset.

Abundance begins in your thinking before it manifests in your living. When your heart and mind come into agreement with Heaven's economy, you begin to attract divine opportunities, favor, and provision.

An abundance mindset declares, "I have everything I need. I am blessed to be a blessing. What God gives me is not just for me, it is to impact the world around me."

Think of yourself as a wellspring, not a reservoir. A reservoir stores; a wellspring overflows. When you cultivate your gifts, talents, and resources with excellence and intention, you will overflow into every environment you enter, pouring out encouragement, wisdom, creativity, and breakthroughs.

"And God is able to make all grace abound toward you; that ye, always having all sufficiency in all things, may abound to every good work."

—2 Corinthians 9:8

These words are not just a promise; they are a prophetic decree over your life. You will abound in every good work, not just spiritually, but mentally, emotionally, financially, and relationally. You are called to live generously, give freely, and serve boldly, not out of lack, but from the overflow of God's abundance within you.

Let this become your declaration:

"I do not shrink. I do not fear lack. I am aligned with the abundance of Heaven. I receive freely, and I give extravagantly. I am blessed, and I am a blessing."

When you embrace an abundance mindset, generosity becomes your lifestyle. You no longer live in fear of running out, because you know your Source is unlimited. You become a distribution center for God's glory, pouring out what Heaven has poured in.

So, open your heart wide. Expand your capacity. Believe big. Sow big. Live big. You are not called to scrape by, you are called to thrive, to bless, and to build.

Key Number 11: Embracing Flexibility, Remaining Open to God's Divine Surprises

Flexibility is a form of spiritual maturity. It is not weakness; it is wisdom. It is the recognition that while we may craft the plan, God writes the blueprint. His thoughts are higher. His timing is perfect. His route may not always make sense, but it is always strategic, sovereign, and supernatural.

We must become like clay in the Potter's hands, moldable, adaptable, and yielded. Flexibility allows God to shape our lives in ways that far exceed our limited expectations. Some of the greatest breakthroughs you will ever experience will come through doors you did not expect to walk through.

Think of it like this: life will stretch you. Like a rubber band in the hands of the Master, He stretches your capacity, not to break you but to build you. Every stretch is preparation for greater impact. Some seasons may feel uncomfortable, unfamiliar, or unpredictable, but those are often the exact places where God performs His most profound miracles.

> *"A man's heart deviseth his way: but the Lord directeth his steps."*
>
> *—Proverbs 16:9*

This verse is a holy reminder: you can plan, but it is God who positions. You can set the direction, but it is God who orders the divine appointments. Stop fearing detours. Some of them are destiny shortcuts. What feels like a delay may be divine redirection.

Here is your declaration:

"Lord, I release my need to control every detail. I trust you. I yield to Your timing, Your route, and Your surprises. I remain flexible in faith,

knowing that every unexpected turn is orchestrated by Your sovereign hand."

Flexibility is not about abandoning your purpose; it is about trusting the process. So stay open. Stay expectant. Stay yielded. The next surprise might be your breakthrough in disguise.

Key Number 12: Embracing Love, Loving Yourself

Before you can fully love others, you must first learn to love yourself the way God loves you. This is not pride; it is alignment. It is divine agreement with the One who formed you, called you, and called you good.

Self-love begins with self-acceptance and choosing to embrace the masterpiece God designed when He made you. You are not a mistake. You are not flawed. You are fearfully and wonderfully made, crafted by the hands of the Master Potter Himself. Every quirk, every scar, every strength, and every perceived shortcoming has purpose.

Remember what Scripture teaches us:

"Shall the clay say to him that fashioneth it, What makest thou?"

—Isaiah 45:9

Absolutely not. Do not insult your Creator by despising His creation, you. Stop rehearsing your inadequacies and start declaring your identity. You are God's workmanship, a vessel of glory, marked by grace.

Here is the truth: You do not need to be perfect. You just need to be present in your purpose. You do not need to impress; just express who God made you to be. When you truly love yourself, comparison dies.

Insecurity flees. Fear loses its grip. You stop looking for validation in others because you have already been affirmed by the One who matters most.

Start cheering for yourself. Encourage yourself like David did. Become your own loudest cheerleader. When you wake up in the morning, speak life over your reflection. Say, "I am chosen. I am equipped. I am worthy. I am enough." Speak those words until your soul believes it.

"Finally, brethren, whatsoever things are true, whatsoever things are honest, whatsoever things are just, whatsoever things are pure, whatsoever things are lovely, whatsoever things are of good report; if there be any virtue, and if there be any praise, think on these things."

—Philippians 4:8

This Scripture is not just a meditation. It is a command to filter your thoughts. That includes the thoughts you have about yourself. If your thoughts do not align with what God says about you, reject them. Replace them. Renew your mind daily with the truth of who you are.

Say this aloud:

"I love who God made me to be. I embrace every part of me. I am a vessel of beauty, purpose, and power. I walk boldly in the love of Christ."

You are God's good report. When He formed you, He looked at you and said, "It is good." Let that truth anchor your identity. Let it transform how you see yourself. Because when you truly love yourself in Christ, you become limitless.

Embracing the Fullness of God's Purpose

Living out your God-given purpose is one of the most powerful and fulfilling journeys you will ever embark upon. However, walking in that divine calling requires more than passion; it demands intentional alignment with Heaven. It means embracing a set of spiritual keys that unlock the fullness of your destiny:

- **Seeking divine guidance**
- **Surrendering control to God's plan**
- **Exercising unwavering patience**
- **Listening for His whispers**
- **Persevering through trials**
- **Walking by faith and not by sight**
- **Stretching beyond your comfort zone**
- **Cultivating daily gratitude**
- **Recognizing the blessings within you**
- **Adopting an abundance mindset to bless others**
- **Remaining flexible through life's detours**
- **Loving yourself as God so powerfully loves you**

As you embrace these principles, know this: you are not walking alone. The same God who designed your purpose is walking beside you, empowering you, guiding your steps, and celebrating every move you make toward destiny.

Remember, your purpose is not defined solely by what you do. It is most deeply revealed in who you become. As you yield your life to God's plan, your heart will begin to reflect His heart. Your hands will begin to do His work. Your life will become a mirror of His glory. So step boldly into the fullness of what God has for you. Heaven is backing you.

Aim Shift 2: Reflecting on Key Areas to Embrace in Your Purpose Bucket

Now that you have set your Purpose goals, it is time to elevate your reflection and apply divine wisdom to the specific areas of your life. In each of your 8 Purpose Buckets, you will embrace the following principles, allowing them to shape your path toward destiny.

Remember, you do not have to apply all twelve keys to every single Purpose Bucket. There will be areas where specific keys lead to breakthrough, while others may require a different approach.

For instance:

- **Guidance:** Where can you seek or offer guidance in each area? Wisdom comes from God, and you are called to seek it and share it. Divine insight is essential as you move forward in each purpose area.

- **Surrendering:** What do you need to release in order to move forward? Surrender is a divine act of trust, acknowledging that God's plan is always higher and better than your own. Let go, and let God do what only He can.

- **Patience:** Where do you need to exercise patience for growth? Patience is not passive; it is actively trusting that God is working behind the scenes. Your breakthrough is coming, but you must wait with expectation and faith.

- **Hearing God's Voice:** How will you remain open to hearing God's voice in every area? You are designed to hear His whispers. Silence the noise around you and listen intently. God is speaking directly to you.

- **Perseverance:** Where do you need to press forward, even when the going gets tough? Perseverance is the force that propels you when everything else says, "Quit." You are stronger than you realize, and you were created to overcome.

- **Faith:** How can you trust in the process and the outcomes, even in uncertainty? Faith is your bridge between where you are and where God is taking you. Trust the unseen and walk boldly by faith.

- **Stepping Out of Your Comfort Zone:** Where are you hesitating to step forward? Your destiny is on the other side of your comfort zone. Challenge yourself to take the leap, knowing that God will meet you there.

- **Blessings:** How can you fully experience the abundant blessings in every area of your life? God has poured His abundance into you. Do not just recognize it, celebrate it. There is a treasure within you, and the world is waiting for it to be revealed.

- **Gratitude:** Where can you cultivate a heart of gratitude in each area? Gratitude shifts your focus and opens the door for more. You cannot access the fullness of your purpose without a heart that gives thanks.

- **Abundance Mindset:** How can you shift your thinking from scarcity to abundance? The enemy wants you to think there is not enough, but God's Kingdom operates in overflow. When you embrace an abundance mindset, you will become a channel of blessings to others.

- **Flexibility:** Where do you need to be more adaptable and open to change? Life is full of surprises, but God is in control of it all. Flexibility is not weakness; it is the strength to bend without breaking. Adjust to God's leading and trust that He is always moving you toward greater purpose.

Love: How will you love and honor yourself as God created you? You are His masterpiece. When you love yourself, you step into the fullness of your divine potential. Embrace who you are, and let that love overflow into every area of your life.

As you reflect on these powerful keys, know this: They will unlock your growth and guide you to thrive within your Purpose Buckets. You are designed for more. Now is the time to take action and live according to the divine blueprint God has set for you.

Are you ready to take action? Let's go.

CHAPTER 3: THRIVING IN YOUR PURPOSE: FIVE GIFTS YOU RECEIVE WHEN YOU START OPERATING BY DESIGN INSTEAD OF DEFAULT

"The seed will thrive as long as it grows."

—Shaasia Nance

You are on fire, Purpose-Driven Friend! You have uncovered your divine assignment. You have embraced it with boldness. Now it is time to move beyond survival into supernatural thriving.

First, let's pause for a moment and ask yourself: What does it truly mean to thrive in your purpose?

To thrive is to live in divine rhythm, aligned, anointed, and activated. It is stepping into a realm where you do not just function, you flourish. Where you are not just busy, but effective. This is where purpose meets destiny and your life becomes a conduit of God's glory.

"For we are his workmanship, created in Christ Jesus unto good works, which God hath before ordained that we should walk in them."

—*Ephesians 2:10*

You are not a mistake. You are not here by accident. You are God's intentional creation, fashioned, formed, and fortified for such a time as this. Your purpose has already been written in the archives of Heaven, and now is your moment to walk it out in full authority.

Let us be clear: thriving is not passive. It is active obedience. It is waking up every day and saying, "Lord, I surrender to the assignment." It is aligning your passions with your purpose, and when that alignment happens, you become unshakable. You become unstoppable. You become a force in the earth.

When you thrive in your purpose, every gift, every sense, every part of your being comes alive. You begin to see more clearly, hear more sharply, discern more deeply, and move with precision.

In this final portion of Part I, we are going to unwrap five divine gifts and spiritual insights tied to your natural senses: sight, hearing, taste, smell, and touch. These are not just physical faculties, they are prophetic portals that God wants to activate in your life to deepen your discernment and sharpen your spiritual edge.

Your sight will be anointed to see beyond the natural.
Your hearing will be tuned to Heaven's frequency.
Your taste will crave the things of God.
Your smell will detect both the fragrance of His presence and the stench of the enemy's deception.
Your touch will carry healing, power, and influence.
You are about to enter a new realm of awareness, where even your senses become weapons of spiritual warfare and instruments of divine purpose.

Get ready to rise. Get ready to rule. Get ready to thrive. Let us unwrap these five gifts and position ourselves to live the abundant, purpose-fueled life God designed from the foundation of the world.

The Five Gifts to Thrive in Your Purpose

Gift #1: Sight, See Beyond What Eyes Can See

Let us begin with the gift of sight, a divine tool through which we not only perceive the world, but also discern the movement of Heaven. Jesus declared in Matthew 6:22–23:

"The light of the body is the eye: if therefore thine eye be single, thy whole body shall be full of light. But if thine eye be evil, thy whole body shall be full of darkness. If therefore the light that is in thee be darkness, how great is that darkness!"

—Matthew 6:22–23

Sight is more than just a physical function, it is a spiritual gateway. What you behold, you become. What you focus on will either illuminate your path or plunge you into confusion. This is why guarding your vision is not optional; it is essential. When your eyes are fixed on God and aligned with His purpose, you move with clarity, strategy, and divine precision. Your steps are ordered. Your spirit is lit with purpose. When your sight is distracted or distorted, you lose focus, and where there is no focus, there is no forward momentum.

"Where there is no vision, the people perish."

—Proverbs 29:18

Purpose requires prophetic vision. You must learn to see as God sees. This is not about your natural eyesight, it is about receiving spiritual insight, discernment, and divine perspective.

How do you steward this gift? Surround yourself with vision-filled reminders. Decorate your atmosphere with declarations of God's Word. Place Scripture on your walls, mirrors, desk, and even your refrigerator. Give your eyes something faith-building to lock onto. These visual cues become prophetic billboards that remind you of Heaven's assignment.

Personally, I have placed Scriptures on Post-it notes in my office, on the bathroom mirror, and on the refrigerator. These are not just decorations, they are spiritual anchors. On days when doubt tries to whisper, these truths shout louder.

Let us dive a little deeper.

> **"The hearing ear, and the seeing eye, the Lord hath made even both of them."**
>
> *—Proverbs 20:12*

Ask God to anoint your eyes, not just your physical eyes, but the eyes of your spirit. Like Elisha prayed for his servant in 2 Kings 6:17, cry out, "Lord, I pray thee, open his eyes, that he may see." See the angel armies. See the victory that already surrounds you. See beyond the battle into breakthrough. See what God is doing even when your circumstances do not reflect it. You were not called to walk blindly. You were born to see with precision, to operate with spiritual intelligence, and to discern your destiny from God's vantage point.

Align your sight.
Sharpen your vision.
Guard what you gaze upon.

Keep your spiritual eyes locked on the One who holds the blueprint for your purpose. This is how you thrive with the gift of sight.

So I decree today:

Your eyes are anointed to see as God sees. You do not walk in blindness. You walk in vision. Your natural sight is submitted to divine perspective. You are not distracted by what you see in the flesh because your spirit sees beyond the surface. You discern movement in the unseen realm. You perceive purpose in the middle of pressure. You see promise even in the midst of the process.

You are a woman of prophetic vision. Your focus is clear. Your gaze is steady. You are not tossed by confusion or clouded by fear. Your eyes are fixed on the Author and Finisher of your faith. You see strategies from Heaven. You see open doors before they appear. You see battles won before they are even fought.

Every lie is being cast down, and every distortion is being corrected. Your sight is aligned. Your vision is sharpened. The eyes of your understanding are enlightened. You no longer chase shadows. You pursue substance. You walk by faith and not by sight, yet your spiritual eyes are wide open.

You will see the hand of God in motion. You will see angels encamped around you. You will see the fulfillment of every promise spoken. Your eyes are healthy, and your whole body is filled with light. From this day forward, you will no longer live confused or distracted. You are seeing clearly and moving purposefully in the direction of your divine destiny.

In Jesus' name, amen.

Gift #2: Hearing, Tune Your Ears to Heaven's Frequency

Let us now unlock the gift of hearing, the divine sense that tunes us into the frequency of Heaven. This is not just about physical sound; this is about spiritual perception and supernatural clarity. Jesus said in John 10:27:

> *"My sheep hear my voice, and I know them, and they follow me."*
>
> *—John 10:27*

To thrive in your purpose, you must become fluent in the language of the Spirit. The world is noisy. Distractions scream. Doubts whisper. Nevertheless, the voice of God comes as a whisper of power, a sacred frequency that cuts through chaos and brings divine instruction.

You must train your ears to discern the difference between noise and the voice of the Lord. The path you are called to walk requires that you hear with accuracy and obey with immediacy.

> *"Be still, and know that I am God."*
>
> *—Psalm 46:10*

In a culture obsessed with volume and busyness, stillness becomes your spiritual superpower. In stillness, you activate your ears. In stillness, you silence fear. In stillness, you hear the strategy of Heaven.

Here is how you cultivate your spiritual hearing: Set aside time daily not just to speak, but to listen. Open the Word and expect God to speak. Enter prayer not as a monologue, but as a divine dialogue. Allow the Holy Spirit to amplify His whisper and bring direction, correction, and confirmation.

There was a season when I woke up early each morning, not to run into the day, but to lean into the voice of God. I would sit in silence and simply ask, "Father, what is my assignment today?" He would speak sometimes through a verse, a word, or even a divine impression. I realized God does not shout because He is far; He whispers because He is near.

> **"And thine ears shall hear a word behind thee, saying, This is the way, walk ye in it."**
>
> *—Isaiah 30:21*

This is not imagination; this is revelation. God is still speaking. The question is: Are you postured to hear?

Hearing God is more than inspiration, it is instruction for destiny. When your ears are tuned to His voice, you do not merely survive, you strategically advance. You walk boldly. You obey instantly. You move prophetically.

Discipline your hearing. Guard your listening in every environment. Shut out the noise of doubt, fear, and the enemy's lies. Lean into the still, small voice that leads you with power.

You cannot thrive in your purpose without divine direction. So posture yourself as a listener. The more you hear, the more clearly you will move in sync with God's divine agenda for your life. This is how you thrive through the gift of hearing.

So I decree today:

Your ears are anointed to hear the voice of the Lord with clarity, confidence, and consistency. You are not confused. You are not distracted. You are not deaf to the Spirit. You are tuned to the frequency of Heaven. The noise of this world no longer overpowers the whisper of God. You are still enough to hear Him and bold enough to obey Him.

The voice of the Good Shepherd leads you daily. You recognize His voice. You follow without hesitation. You obey without delay. Every instruction you need for your next season has already been released in the secret place. You are a woman who listens with precision and moves with purpose.

You will not follow the voice of fear. You will not follow the voice of doubt. You will not follow the lies of the enemy. You will follow the voice of truth. You will walk in divine strategy, divine timing, and divine alignment.

Today, your spiritual ears are open. Your heart is receptive. Your steps are ordered. You hear with clarity. You move with confidence. You respond with obedience. And because of that, you are advancing in your God-given assignment with supernatural accuracy.

In Jesus' name, amen.

Gift #3: Taste – Feasting on the Goodness of God

Now, let's consider the divine gift of taste. Psalm 34:8 declares:

> **"O taste and see that the Lord is good: blessed is the man that trusteth in him."**
>
> *—Psalm 34:8*

This is more than poetic language; it is a personal invitation into experience. Just as we savor the richness of a gourmet meal, we are called to taste the depth of God's goodness, His faithfulness, and His divine provision. This kind of tasting isn't passive; it's intentional. It's about feasting daily on the truth of God's Word, allowing it to satisfy your soul and fuel your assignment. When you taste Him, you'll never hunger for counterfeit substitutes again. The more you feed on His presence, the more your appetite is refined, purified, and set ablaze for the things of the Kingdom.

How do you use this sense to thrive in your purpose? You nourish your spirit. You sit at the feet of Jesus and dine on revelation. You partake in communion not just as a ritual but as a reminder that your strength, your sustenance, your strategy all flow from the finished work of the Cross. Fellowship with believers becomes a feast of encouragement, sharpening, and divine alignment.

Jesus said in John 6:35:

> ***"I am the bread of life: he that cometh to me shall never hunger."***
>
> ***—John 6:35***

This is your promise: when you come to Him daily, expectantly, you will be filled with everything you need to walk boldly in your purpose. I've learned that when I start my day in the Word, it changes the taste of my entire day. My spiritual cravings are aligned. I do not chase empty calories; I feast on the Bread of Life. With every bite, I'm strengthened, filled, and propelled toward destiny.

Let your taste be refined for His goodness. Crave the things of Heaven. Digest the Word until it becomes a part of you. When you truly taste and see that He is good, you'll be unshakable and unmistakably thriving in your purpose. This is how you thrive through the gift of taste.

So I decree today:

Your spiritual appetite is shifting. You no longer crave what is empty, fleeting, or false. You hunger for righteousness. You feast on the faithfulness of God. Your soul is satisfied by the Bread of Life, and your spirit is nourished by fresh revelation from Heaven.

You are a woman who dines daily at the table of the Lord. The Word is your sustenance. His presence is your portion. His goodness is your delight. You taste, and you see that the Lord is good. And because of that, you walk in clarity, fullness, and divine strength.

You are not weak. You are well-fed. You are not chasing crumbs. You are seated at the King's table. Every day, your cravings are aligned with your calling. From this place of spiritual nourishment, you rise. You speak with authority. You move with grace. You thrive with purpose.

In Jesus' name, amen.

Gift #4: Smell: Releasing the Fragrance of Christ

Next, let's unpack the gift of smell, a powerful and often overlooked sense that awakens memory, atmosphere, and presence.

In 2 Corinthians 2:15, Paul writes:

"For we are unto God a sweet savour of Christ, in them that are saved, and in them that perish."

—2 Corinthians 2:15

Your life, when surrendered to God's purpose, carries a fragrance, one that reaches Heaven and touches earth. This is not about perfume or outward presentation. This is a spiritual aroma. When you walk in purpose, in alignment, and in the anointing, your very presence begins to shift atmospheres. You carry the scent of the Savior. You release the incense of intimacy. You leave behind traces of love, power, peace, and purpose, and the world takes notice.

How do you cultivate this gift to thrive in your purpose? You immerse yourself in Christ until His fragrance becomes yours. Let His Word soak into your soul until you exude compassion, truth, and holiness. Let your life emit the aroma of integrity, worship, and surrender. As incense rises before the throne, let your life be a constant offering, a living sacrifice of sweet-smelling worship.

Just like a rich fragrance lingers in a room long after someone has gone, your actions, your words, and your spirit leave a lasting imprint. Gratitude and joy become your perfume. Forgiveness becomes your scent. Mercy becomes the air you carry. I have learned that when I spend time in the secret place, I walk out smelling like Heaven. That scent, that glory, goes with me into every space I enter. When you allow God to refine you, the old scent of fear, shame, and brokenness is replaced with the fresh fragrance of purpose, healing, and hope. This is how you thrive through the gift of smell.

So I decree today:

You are the aroma of Christ. You carry the scent of victory, the fragrance of fire-tested faith, and the sweet smell of destiny. Your life carries the aroma of Heaven. You are the fragrance of Christ in the earth. You walk into rooms and shift atmospheres with the scent of worship, purity, and divine presence. Fear cannot linger where you dwell. Darkness cannot hide where you stand. The aroma of your obedience releases healing. The fragrance of your faith releases breakthroughs.

You do not carry the scent of shame, failure, or fear. You have been washed, refined, and anointed. You smell like surrender. You smell like victory. You smell like oil that has been crushed and consecrated for the King's use. Your words release the fragrance of wisdom. Your actions leave the scent of compassion. Your worship rises as sweet incense before the throne.

Today, may your life leave a lasting imprint, a trail of peace, joy, mercy, and truth. May your presence be proof that you have been in the presence of God. Even after you leave a place, may the residue of His glory remain.

You are a living offering. A walking altar. A sweet aroma rising to Heaven. Everywhere you go, others will know you have been with Jesus.

In Jesus' name, amen.

Gift #5: Touch: The Power to Heal, Restore, and Activate Destiny

Finally, we arrive at the gift of touch, the divine ability to connect, comfort, and catalyze transformation. In Acts 17:27, Paul declares:

> **"That they should seek the Lord, if haply they might feel after him, and find him, though he be not far from every one of us: for in him we live, and move, and have our being."**
>
> **—Acts 17:27–28**

Touch is more than a physical gesture. It is the manifestation of God's love in motion. It is how Heaven reaches earth through human hands. When you touch someone's life with kindness, compassion, prayer, or presence, you become the hands and feet of Jesus. You extend His heart to the broken, His healing to the hurting, and His love to the lonely. Touch carries power and purpose.

So, how can you activate this sacred sense to thrive in your calling? Reach out. Hug someone who feels invisible. Hold the hand of someone walking through grief. Write words that touch hearts. Serve with humility. Let every action be anointed with divine intentionality. Each morning, I ask God, "Whose life can I touch today?" It might be through a kind word, a heartfelt prayer, a meal shared, or even the words you're reading right now. As I pour out what God has poured into me, I see lives shift. Your voice, your gift, your obedience touches more than you know.

One birthday, I created a kindness challenge. I split a list of good deeds between my friends and family, and together we blessed dozens of strangers. That day, I did not just celebrate life. I became a conduit of revival through compassion. It was one of the most powerful birthdays I have ever experienced, and a reminder that one touch from God, through you, can change everything.

Reflect: When was the last time someone's words, hug, or generosity reminded you that God sees you? Now go be that for someone else. Whether it is through a prayer, a text, a smile, or a word, your touch activates healing, your presence releases hope, and your obedience unlocks purpose. This is how you thrive in the gift of touch.

So I decree today:

Your touch is anointed with purpose. Your hands are consecrated to carry healing, compassion, and power. You are the hands and feet of Jesus in the earth. Every word you speak, every act of kindness you offer, every moment of presence you extend releases Heaven into the lives of others.

You are not just a woman of prayer. You are a vessel of impact. Your hugs break heaviness. Your prayers pierce through pain. Your presence carries peace. God moves through you to comfort the grieving, uplift the weary, and remind the overlooked that they are seen, known, and loved.

Your hands build. Your voice restores. Your obedience opens doors. What you release through love today has the power to shift atmospheres and break chains. You are not limited by your reach, because the anointing on your life extends beyond your physical touch. Even your words carry weight. Your compassion creates revival.

Today, you rise as a carrier of hope. You serve with humility. You love with intention. You show up with purpose. You do not just go through life. You touch lives with the power of God flowing through you.

In Jesus' name, amen.

As we close this journey, remember this truth: You are fully equipped. God has gifted you with the senses of sight, hearing, taste, smell, and touch not just for survival, but for supernatural impact. Each sense, when surrendered to God, becomes a tool for transformation.

You are called to see with clarity, hear with discernment, taste His goodness, carry the fragrance of Christ, and touch lives with power and purpose. You are not ordinary. You are a vessel of glory, a divine expression of His purpose in the earth.

So I declare over you:

Arise, beautiful friend of God. Activate your senses. Walk boldly in your calling. Thrive in the fullness of your purpose.

Aim Shift 3: Activate Divine Alignment Through Your Senses

Take a pause and reflect on how each of your God-given senses, sight, hearing, taste, smell, and touch, can become portals to deeper intimacy with the Father. These are not just physical faculties; they are spiritual instruments that tune you into the rhythm of Heaven and align you with God's divine strategy for your life.

As you intentionally seek Him with every sense, you will begin to experience His purpose in a whole new dimension. You will see with clarity, hear with divine discernment, taste His faithfulness, carry the fragrance of Christ, and touch lives with Kingdom authority.

This is your aim shift. You will no longer live by natural instinct alone. Instead, you will operate with heightened awareness of the Spirit. Embrace this activation. Let it transform how you experience God and how you walk in your purpose.

You are not wandering. You are walking with divine precision.

Part 2: Ladder

A ladder is more than a tool; it is a symbol of divine elevation. It represents access, ascension, and advancement. Just as a ladder is designed to help someone climb higher, so God has placed ladders in your life to help you rise into the fullness of your destiny. Nothing in your life is random; every rung is intentional, every step is prophetic, every climb is purposed.

A physical ladder allows you to reach places that were previously inaccessible. In the spirit, the ladder represents supernatural strategies, divine appointments, kingdom connections, and moments of obedience that propel you into realms of breakthrough. It is not by might, nor by power, but by the Spirit of the living God that you ascend!

You were not created to remain stagnant. You were designed to go from faith to faith, from strength to strength, from glory to glory. Just like Jacob's ladder in Genesis 28, which connected Heaven to earth, your life is a conduit for divine activity. Angels ascend and descend on your behalf. Doors open. Portals unlock. Dimensions shift. You climb not in your own strength, but with the wind of God beneath your feet.

Every rung you step on declares: Elevation is your portion. Breakthrough is your inheritance. Access has been granted.

So rise, daughter of God. Climb with confidence. Heaven is backing you. You are anointed to go higher.

CHAPTER 4: POSITIONING YOUR LADDER IS THE KEY TO MAKING SURE YOU ARE CLIMBING TOWARD PURPOSE, NOT JUST SUCCESS

"Position your tools to achieve success."

—*Shaasia Nance*

Hey, sis, listen up. You were not just born to dream, you were born to do it. You were born to rise. You were born to build. Now it is time to map out the strategy that Heaven has already written over your life.

You have God-sized goals, purpose-anchored, legacy-leaving, destiny-defining goals, and now it is time to break them down into action steps that align with the anointing on your life. Here is the beauty of it all: you are not building this ladder alone. Jehovah Jireh, your Provider, El Elyon, your Most High God, is building with you, beside you, and within you.

> *"Except the Lord build the house, they labour in vain that build it."*
>
> —*Psalm 127:1*

Let us talk about this ladder. Each rung represents a small but intentional step, an obedient act, a faith-filled move toward the higher place God is calling you to. In the last few chapters, you outlined your purpose goals across eight divine categories. Now it is time to build upward. Each step, or "rung," must be laid with prayer, clarity, and strategic obedience.

Now, sis, hear me in the Spirit: faith is not passive. It is active, bold, and courageous. Faith is the fire that fuels our forward motion, but faith without action is like prophecy without obedience: useless, fruitless, dormant.

> *"Even so faith, if it hath not works, is dead, being alone."*
>
> *—James 2:17*

Think about Noah. He did not just believe God, he built. Think about the woman with the issue of blood. She did not just hope for healing, she reached. Think about Joshua. He did not just hear the command, he crossed over.

Each story is a divine blueprint: faith matched with movement releases miracles.

Beloved, climbing your ladder requires courage. It demands that you make moves even when the next rung feels shaky. Proverbs 3:5–6 is your guide here:

> *"Trust in the Lord with all thine heart; and lean not unto thine own understanding. In all thy ways acknowledge him, and he shall direct thy paths."*
>
> *—Proverbs 3:5–6*

You do not need all the details, you need divine direction. When your steps are ordered by God, you can move forward with supernatural confidence, knowing Heaven backs your yes. This is the season to submit your strategy in prayer, then move your feet in power. You are not just creating action steps, you are activating kingdom assignments. Do not just be a woman of vision, be a woman of execution. Write the vision, yes. Pray over the plan, yes. But sis, move. This is the chapter where we silence fear, cast down procrastination, and climb with power.

"Now faith is the substance of things hoped for, the evidence of things not seen."

—Hebrews 11:1

So even when you do not see the full picture, even when the resources have not shown up yet, even when the door seems closed, move. Move like it is already open. Move like the ladder is already secured. Move like God already said yes. Because He did.

My Story on Ascending the Ladder

On my journey to living out my God-given purpose, I realized I was not taking the right steps toward my destiny because I was waiting for giant leaps in life. I kept waiting for the perfect moment, the right time, the right people, and the right opportunities. As I waited, I found myself stuck in the same cycle, repeating the same patterns day after day. I prayed, stayed faithful to God's Word, and waited for Him to move on my behalf. Yet, my life still felt unfulfilled.

It was not until God revealed that I needed to take small, intentional steps that I began to make real progress. I started writing down my ladder steps and following through. Suddenly, my life began to change in what felt like the blink of an eye. I had not realized how powerful those small steps truly were. The Bible tells us not to despise small beginnings, and those words became real to me. Each small step moved me closer to living out my dreams. I launched a business, started a TV show, created a women's conference, and even began a hair care line. It was as if all my blessings opened up simply because I took consistent, simple actions.

As I climbed each rung of the ladder, I accomplished more in three months than I had in years. For the first time, I truly felt alive. I was living my purpose, not someone else's. I was chasing my dreams, aligned with God's divine plan for my life. Every day, I woke up hungry for what God had in store, eager to learn more. I took my little steps, knowing every second, minute, and hour mattered. Those moments turned into days, weeks, months, and years, and those small actions turned into TV shows, books, conferences, and businesses. Every step mattered.

As I wrote down each step on my ladder, I made sure they aligned with God's path for me. I know God moves according to His Word and promises because He is faithful. Knowing His faithfulness motivated me to be faithful in following through. I did not write my ladder steps just to let them sit on paper. I committed to discipline, refusing to let distractions pull me off course.

This reminds me of Nehemiah, who was rebuilding the wall and refused to come down. He was too focused on his purpose to be distracted by old ways or doubts. He was on a new journey and would not stop until the work was done. Likewise, I encourage you not to let anything or anyone distract you on your ladder. God is with you, cheering you on.

"If God be for us, who can be against us?"

—Romans 8:31

Stay focused. Do not shrink. Do not look back. Keep climbing with your eyes fixed on God, Heaven's spotlight shining on you!

Mapping Out My Ladder

Mapping out my ladder helped me discern which opportunities truly aligned with my purpose. I now understand that even though some opportunities seem amazing, they might not be right for me. My pastor once said, "Just because something is good doesn't mean you should always pursue it." I turned down many good opportunities because they did not fit my God-given purpose.

One of my biggest distractions was my passion for helping others. I tried so hard to build other people's dreams that I neglected my own. God showed me that if I stayed focused on my own path first, I could eventually help thousands, not just a few. It was a hard lesson because my heart is to serve, but if I do not climb my ladder first, I can't lead others up theirs. If I'm stuck at the bottom, I can't help anyone else up.

Imagine trying to climb a ladder while carrying your friends and family. It might sound noble, but it's impossible. Each step gets harder, and eventually, you'll lose your footing. But if you climb with God, you can pave the way for others to follow. Imagine climbing the ladder with your friends and family right behind you or beside you, much easier than carrying them all at once. When you reach the top, you can help thousands, even millions, teaching them how to climb their own ladders.

Now, I am able to help more people than ever before because those daily small steps helped me focus, organize my efforts, and say "no" to opportunities that do not align with my purpose. Those possibilities came through climbing my ladder with God.

As you begin to climb toward your God-ordained goals, remember this, you are never alone. God walks with you every step of the way, ready to pour out His wisdom, guidance, and supernatural strength exactly when you need it most.

"Commit thy works unto the Lord, and thy thoughts shall be established."

—Proverbs 16:3

When you surrender your dreams and your steps to God, inviting Him into every part of your journey, He doesn't just bless your efforts, He establishes your path and orders your steps toward success.

So as you write down those specific ladder steps to reach your goals, make sure you include God in every detail. Carve out time each day to pray, to seek His wisdom, His clarity, and His direction. And don't hold back from stepping out boldly in faith, trusting that God will open doors, create opportunities, and make a way where there seems to be no way.

Keep your eyes fixed on Him and His promises.

"Fear thou not; for I am with thee: be not dismayed; for I am thy God: I will strengthen thee; yea, I will help thee; yea, I will uphold thee with the right hand of my righteousness."

—Isaiah 41:10

Let these words cast out every fear and doubt. Stand firm in the confidence that comes from knowing God is not only on your side, He is carrying you.

Every year, as I prepared for the new school year, I focused on designing my classroom, buying furniture and supplies I thought would make it perfect for my students. One day, while adding items to my Amazon cart, the Lord spoke to me: "Don't purchase anything. You'll be switching positions before the year ends. Prepare for an office." I obeyed and didn't buy anything for my classroom.

Fast forward to the end of the school year, an ideal position opened up that seemed perfect. It aligned with my interests and felt like a step toward my goals. During prayer, God reminded me of my purpose, my buckets, and my ladder. Reviewing my ladder, I realized this job didn't align with my actionable steps or purpose. The more I learned about it, the more I discerned it would consume too much of my time and distract me from family and current responsibilities.

So, I declined the job. A week later, during my lunch break, I sought God's clarity and found a position perfectly aligned with His vision, but it required transferring districts.

As I prepared to apply, I prayed for God's direction. Minutes later, a coworker told me she was transferring, and the position she was leaving was exactly the one I was just about to apply for in the other district. God had opened the door right where I was. Had I not followed my ladder and purpose, I would have missed this opportunity. God's faithfulness showed up in His perfect timing.

This experience reinforced how vital it is to involve God in every part of your plan. He will give you the wisdom to choose the right path and the strength to remain faithful to it.

So climb with courage, my sister. Your ladder is more than a plan, it's a journey of faith, empowered by the One who holds the universe in His hands. The victory is yours.

Are You Ready To Climb This Ladder?

So, sis, you are probably wondering how you actually climb this ladder of goals God has placed in your heart. It starts with clarity and strategy.

Remember those beautiful purpose goals you identified in Part 1? Those are your signposts, your divine checkpoints, guiding you on this journey. Now it is time to break each goal down into bite-sized, manageable steps. Just like climbing a ladder, you take it one rung at a time, one intentional move after another.

Do not be afraid to get granular here. The more specific your action plan, the sharper your focus, and the stronger your motivation. Write down each ladder step with clear milestones to hold yourself accountable. Use whatever tools work for you, a to-do list, a calendar, or even a project management app. The key is to stay organized and keep your eyes on the prize.

Set aside time each week to review your progress and adjust your plan as God directs. And listen, celebrate every single victory, no matter how small. Each step forward is a testament to God's faithfulness and your obedience.

"And whatsoever ye do, do it heartily, as to the Lord, and not unto men; knowing that of the Lord ye shall receive the reward of the inheritance: for ye serve the Lord Christ."

—Colossians 3:23-24

Building your ladder this way shows you are not just busy, you are strategic, intentional, and wholehearted about walking in your God-ordained purpose.

One of the greatest benefits of this approach is that it builds momentum and confidence. Every small step is a victory that reinforces your belief in your ability to overcome and succeed. When challenges come (and they will), you will draw strength from the progress you have already made, knowing you have what it takes to keep moving forward.

But here is the real power: breaking your goals into manageable steps keeps you focused and clear amid life's chaos. You can face each day with purpose and intention, knowing exactly what needs to be done to move closer to your dreams.

So, grab that pen and paper. Write down those specific steps. Map out your path with faith and precision. Then step out boldly into the adventure God has prepared for you. The best is yet to come, and God is right there beside you.

Aim Shift 4: Break It Down into Manageable Steps

Now it is time to zoom in and break your goals into small, manageable steps. For each category under your purpose goal buckets, list your specific ladder steps. These should be simple actions that will move you closer to your goals.

These steps do not need to be big or complicated. For example, if your goal is to build stronger relationships with family, a small action under your ladder could be: Text my grandma every Thursday. It might seem minor, but over time, this consistent habit will deepen your connection much more than only catching up during family gatherings.

For every purpose goal you have written down, ask yourself: What can I do right now? These steps do not have to be perfect. They can and should evolve as you grow and progress. The key is to have a clear plan with actionable steps that help you steadily climb your ladder toward your purpose. As you take each small step, you will find yourself moving forward consistently, building momentum and confidence in your journey.

Next, you are going to reflect and align. Take intentional time to pray over your list. Ask God for clear guidance and wisdom. Seek His voice to make sure the steps you have planned line up with His purpose for your life. Be open to any shifts or new directions He may reveal. Sometimes God shows us better paths or refines our actions. Do not resist the adjustments.

After prayer, revisit your list with fresh eyes and a soft heart. Willingness to revise is a sign of growth and trust in God's leadership. Let this process bring you peace and confidence. You are not just making plans. Again, you are aligning with God's divine plan.

Remember: His timing and direction are perfect. Keep trusting, keep praying, and keep stepping forward with faith.

CHAPTER 5: BEING DILIGENT ON YOUR LADDER MEANS STAYING FOCUSED, FAITHFUL, AND FRUITFUL NO MATTER THE LEVEL YOU'RE ON

"The best partner to climb with is God."

—*Shaasia Nance*

Diligence is not just about working hard, it is about being fiercely focused, relentlessly persistent, and spiritually grounded. It is steady, earnest, and energetic effort, a sacred devotion that fuels destiny. Diligence is what keeps you climbing when life tries to knock you down. It is the holy fire that burns within the committed.

Keep a Diligent Mindset When Climbing

Hey, my beautiful sister, you must armor your mind with diligence. Stay steady. Stay faithful. Stay locked into the divine blueprint Heaven has already drawn up for your life. Hear this: You must make a non-negotiable decision in your spirit to remain supernaturally focused.

That is why mindset is the master key. Of all the eight purpose buckets, mindset is the one you must guard with everything you have. When your mind is aligned with the Spirit of God, everything else flows. When your mind is cluttered, confused, or compromised, your destiny becomes delayed.

To be diligent is to wage war against every lie, limitation, and label. You must create a plan to protect your mental gates. Your thoughts shape your words. Your words shape your world. So take dominion over your thought life. Take territory over every thought through the Blood of Jesus.

> *"And be not conformed to this world: but be ye transformed by the renewing of your mind, that ye may prove what is that good, and acceptable, and perfect, will of God."*

> *—Romans 12:2*

Transformation does not begin with your circumstances, it begins with your thinking. Every day, declare war on fear, anxiety, and confusion. Declare: "My mind is fortified. My thoughts are anointed. My focus is unbreakable. My destiny is non-negotiable."

Every promise, every prayer, every prophetic word God has spoken over your life, meditate on it daily. You are rewiring your brain, rewriting your patterns, and reclaiming your mental territory. Science confirms what the Word already revealed: you can literally reprogram your brain. So imagine what could happen if you devoted just 365 days to transforming your mindset. One year of intentional, Spirit-led thinking can catapult you into another dimension.

One year, I committed to becoming a new woman from the inside out, and I did. More joy. More peace. More power. More clarity. Not by accident, but by assignment. Each day, I decided to change my mindset and step into everything that God has promised me. I made a commitment to myself: 365 days from now, I was going to be different. My mind would become more fortified, more resilient.

As I embarked on this 365-day Beautiful Mind Challenge, I noticed a transformation. I had more joy, more peace, more love, and more hope. This challenge turned out to be the most life-changing experience for me. By taking time each day to focus on renewing my mind, I saw just how much I could accomplish in a year. Small, daily shifts in mindset can lead to huge changes over time.

Start today. Commit to your next 365-day transformation. Do not just exist, elevate. Each new morning is an opportunity to honor the life God gave you by thinking higher. You are not allowed to come down. No retreat. No surrender. No self-sabotage.

The ladder you are climbing is divine. Every rung takes you closer to your assignment, your anointing, your next level.

So climb, my sister.
Climb past the noise.
Climb past the pain.
Climb until your mindset matches your mantle.
Climb until Heaven looks down and says, "That is My daughter, faithful and focused."

"I can do all things through Christ which strengtheneth me."

—Philippians 4:13

You are fortified. You are focused. You are fierce. Stay diligent. Keep climbing. Be diligent about the words you speak to yourself. Do not mentally abuse yourself, mentally affirm yourself. Speak life. Speak healing. Speak breakthrough. Remove the foxes and release the fruit of the Spirit.

"Take us the foxes, the little foxes, that spoil the vines:"

—Song of Solomon 2:15

Those little foxes, self-sabotaging thoughts, inner critics, negative cycles must be evicted from your mental vineyard. You cannot afford to let fear, insecurity, or doubt eat away at your fruitfulness.

"And the second is like unto it, Thou shalt love thy neighbour as thyself."

—Matthew 22:39

Let me ask you this: Have you loved yourself diligently? Because until you treat yourself with the same compassion, patience, and love you give others, you will keep pouring from an empty vessel.

Learn to Love YOURSELF.

Diligence in Action

My sister, when it comes to climbing your ladder, diligence is your divine fuel. It is the oil that keeps your lamp burning through late nights, difficult seasons, and unseen labor.

"The thoughts of the diligent tend only to plenteousness; but of every one that is hasty only to want."

—Proverbs 21:5

That is not just a Scripture, it is a promise. Steady persistence produces supernatural results. Just like a farmer faithfully tending crops, you must nurture your God-given dreams with care, commitment, and consistency. Maybe your work feels mundane, repetitive, or like it is just a means to an end. But the Word of God gives us a Heavenly perspective:

> *"And whatsoever ye do, do it heartily, as to the Lord, and not unto men; knowing that of the Lord ye shall receive the reward of the inheritance: for ye serve the Lord Christ."*
>
> —*Colossians 3:23-24*

Your job is not just a paycheck. It is an altar. Every task, every email sent, every room cleaned, every patient helped, every diaper changed is an opportunity to worship with excellence. Your labor becomes a love offering to the Lord.

Shift your mindset. What if that small task was sacred? What if every ordinary assignment was actually divine? When you see it this way, everything changes. You will stop chasing recognition and start living with Kingdom intention.

To work heartily means you give your best, not for applause, but because He is watching and rewarding. It is how you carry yourself when no one is watching. It is how you respond under pressure. It is how you serve others with love, grace, and integrity.

You are God's ambassador in every space you step into, your job, your home, your school, your business. He is reflected through your diligence. And let us not forget what Paul says. The reward is eternal. You are not just working for a promotion. You are working for a Heavenly inheritance. That is where the peace comes in, the kind that passeth all understanding. That is where the confidence rises up because you know your labor is never wasted when it is done for Him.

So I ask you: Why are you where you are? Whether you are teaching students, caring for loved ones, building a brand, or managing a home, you have been strategically planted. This is not random. This is not meaningless. It is your mission field.

I remember when this revelation changed my life. Work used to feel like a routine. Just another thing to check off the list. When I realized that every moment was a ministry opportunity, everything shifted. Even the smallest things took on eternal value. Helping a coworker. Sending an encouraging note. Cleaning up after a long day. It all became holy.

This mindset transformed the way I teach, the way I lead, the way I serve. My classroom became my platform. My work became my witness.

You may not always see the fruit, but do not be deceived, you are sowing seeds. Every kind word. Every act of patience. Every moment of obedience. Heaven is recording it all. Your light is piercing the darkness, for your students, your coworkers, your clients, your children. You are pointing people back to Christ simply by showing up with love and purpose.

So stand boldly on Colossians 3:23-24. Let your work become a platform for God's glory. Let every assignment become an opportunity to shine, serve, and sow into eternity.

Let this be your reminder. You were called for this. You matter. Your presence matters. Your diligence matters. Whether you are in a classroom, a hospital room, a boardroom, or a kitchen, you are fulfilling a divine assignment. You are part of a bigger plan, and your obedience is building something eternal.

Keep showing up. Keep pressing forward. Chase your goals with faith, diligence, and Holy Spirit fire. And trust this:

"But Jesus beheld them, and said unto them, With men this is impossible; but with God all things are possible."

—Matthew 19:26

Now rise up and walk it out. Heaven's spotlight is on you!

Diligent in Not Looking Back

Sis, hear me now, Paul declares in Scripture that he forgets what is behind and presses forward toward what lies ahead. This is the mindset of a victorious believer. You must reach. You must climb that ladder. Do not dare look back. You cannot ascend while staring at the ground behind you. Fix your gaze forward, full of faith and expectation, toward the high calling God has placed upon your life.

God designed you for this moment. He fashioned you for this season. You were born to shift atmospheres and transform your world. You are destined for greatness. Climb, and do not look back. Be diligent in shedding the chains of yesterday. The past is a weight, a distraction, a snare meant to slow you down, but you are called to move forward, one steadfast step at a time.

"Brethren, I count not myself to have apprehended: but this one thing I do, forgetting those things which are behind, and reaching forth unto those things which are before,"

—Philippians 3:13

This is your mandate to refuse the lies of failure, to reject the power of regret, and to lock your eyes on your God-ordained destiny.

When your eyes fix on the rung just above, you move forward with divine purpose. If you keep looking down or behind, you lose your balance and risk falling. Picture yourself at the base of that ladder, burdened with regrets, doubts, and wounds. But understand this, those weights are not yours to carry any longer. Release them now. Let go, because you cannot ascend with that dead weight dragging you down.

That ladder is not just wood and metal, it is the stairway to your spiritual breakthrough, your growth, your promotion. Each step is ordained by God, moving you closer to His plan for your life. But here is the absolute truth: you cannot climb while looking back. You must keep your focus on the prize, the high calling that God has engraved on your heart.

Expect distractions. The enemy will tempt you to retreat to old habits, to replay failures, to listen to lies. But God's voice calls louder. He calls you to trust Him fully and press forward, step by step, rung by rung.

So take that next step, be flexible and bold, stand firm in faith, and watch as every obstacle melts before you. You will reach those lofty goals because God's power is working mightily within you.

Aim Shift 5: Renew Your Mindset for Diligence

Now it is time to pause and reflect deeply on your mindset. Ask yourself: What thoughts, attitudes, or habits are holding you back from living fully positive and God-focused? What lies, doubts, or distractions have stealthily crept in to steal your joy and derail your purpose? Identify those strongholds of negativity and self-doubt, and prepare to release them. You must let go of anything that hinders your diligent pursuit of God's calling on your life.

Here are powerful steps to sharpen your focus and align your mind with God's truth:

- *Identify Negative Thought Patterns:* Recognize any recurring negative thoughts that do not serve your destiny or your faith. These are doubts, fears, and distractions that pull you away from your God-ordained goals. Name them, confront them, and reject their power over you.

- *Practice Gratitude Daily:* Shift your focus from what is wrong to what is right. Every morning, thank God for His specific blessings in your life, no matter how small they may seem. This simple practice rewires your mind for positivity and roots you firmly in a God-centered perspective.

- *Release Unnecessary Worries:* Ask yourself: Are the things I am worrying about within my control, or are they burdens I need to surrender to God? Trust fully in His timing and provision. Lay down those heavy loads that were never meant for you to carry alone. on

Reflect On These Questions

- How does this task align with my greater purpose and long-term vision?

- What specific action can I take today to move closer to my God-given destiny?

- Am I dedicating enough focused, undistracted time each day to what truly matters? If not, what shifts must I make?

- What distractions or obstacles could try to block my progress today, and how will I overcome them?

- Am I tracking my progress consistently? What milestones have I reached, and what is my next move?

- What one thing can I do right now that will create the biggest impact on my overall goal?

- How am I staying disciplined even when the work feels hard or tedious?

- What sacrifices or trade-offs am I willing to make to stay faithful to my purpose?

- How do I maintain consistency in my efforts without burning out?

- What new habits or routines can I create to strengthen my diligence and keep me moving forward?

Part 3: Affirming

Affirming is the sacred act of validating, empowering, and uplifting. It means to recognize, endorse, and speak life into the truth of who someone is or what they are doing. To affirm is to strengthen identity, to offer words that reassure the soul, and to build confidence from the inside out.

Affirmation is not just about approval, it is about reinforcement. It intentionally highlights what is good, right, and true. It is a spiritual tool that reinforces a person's value, purpose, and progress. Whether spoken over yourself or someone else, affirming words become seeds that cultivate inner growth and resilience.

In a world full of criticism and comparison, affirmation helps silence the noise of negativity. It promotes a deep sense of God-given worth, reminding you, and those around you, that you are walking in the right direction. It empowers you to keep going, to rise higher, and to believe again.

CHAPTER 6: AFFIRMING YOURSELF IN GOD'S WORD IS HOW YOU REPLACE SELF-DOUBT WITH UNSHAKABLE IDENTITY AND CONFIDENCE

"Beauty is expressed through your words."

—Shaasia Nance

Hello, my beautiful friend of God! You are not an accident. You are not overlooked. You are not forgotten. You are chosen, appointed, and anointed for such a time as this. In this chapter, we will activate the divine authority of God's Word through the discipline of affirmation, not weak, wishful thinking, but powerful declarations rooted in Heaven's truth about who you are.

As you decree the Word of God, you are not just repeating Scripture, you are legislating in the spirit realm. You are aligning your mouth with God's mouth, your thoughts with His thoughts, and your identity with His eternal plan for your life. When you affirm yourself in God's Word, you establish His truth as the foundation of your mindset, your emotions, and your destiny.

The Word of God is alive. It is sharper than any two-edged sword. When you speak it over your life, it cuts through the lies of the enemy, uproots seeds of fear and insecurity, and plants you in the soil of divine confidence and purpose.

Romans 10:17 reminds us:

> *"So then faith cometh by hearing, and hearing by the word of God."*
>
> *—Romans 10:17*

That means the more you speak His truth over your life, the more your faith rises. The more you decree His promises, the more your life aligns with His plan.

When you open your mouth and declare, "I am fearfully and wonderfully made," you silence the voice of shame. When you say, "I am the head and not the tail," you break agreement with inferiority. When you decree, "I can do all things through Christ," you demolish the lie of limitation.

Take this seriously, woman of valor. Make daily affirmations a non-negotiable kingdom discipline. Saturate your heart with Scriptures that declare your worth, your identity, and your divine assignment. Let the Word be your mirror. Look into it and see yourself as Heaven sees you, bold, beautiful, equipped, and empowered.

Your mind is fertile ground. Either you will plant truth, or the enemy will plant lies. Choose today to cultivate a garden of faith. Fill your atmosphere with Scripture. Walk through your house and speak life. Sit with your Bible and declare every promise out loud until it echoes in your spirit.

You are not affirming yourself because you are enough on your own, you are affirming that Christ in you is more than enough. When your words align with His Word, breakthrough is inevitable.

Now, rise up. Speak up. And affirm yourself in God's Word with holy confidence. This is how you walk in dominion. This is how you shift atmospheres. This is how you step into the fullness of who you are.

Decree it. Believe it. Walk in it.

What Are Affirmations? A Kingdom Strategy for Transformation

Affirmations are not just positive statements, they are prophetic declarations and decrees, spoken with authority to establish Heaven's will in the earth. They are spiritual seeds sown into the fertile soil of your mind, and when watered with faith, they grow into trees of righteousness and gardens of divine confidence. They bear fruit in every season, fruit that cannot be shaken by storms, opposition, or delay.

At their core, affirmations are declarations of faith in action. They are bold proclamations rooted in the unshakable promises of God. When you speak affirmations that align with the Word of God, you are not just talking, you are activating. You are reinforcing your belief in God's goodness, His unchanging nature, and His supernatural power to shift your life in real time. Affirmations are one of Heaven's strategies for mind renewal. The Apostle Paul reminds us:

"And be not conformed to this world: but be ye transformed by the renewing of your mind, that ye may prove what is that good, and acceptable, and perfect, will of God."

—Romans 12:2

That renewal begins with what we allow ourselves to believe and speak. When we consistently declare the truth of God's Word, we dismantle strongholds, disarm lies, and rebuild mental frameworks based on faith, not fear. As we learned in the previous chapters.

Let's be clear: the enemy is a liar. He is relentless in his attempts to whisper deception, plant insecurity, and spread doubt. When you rise up and declare, "I am more than a conqueror," you do not just defend yourself, you go on the offensive. Your affirmations become a fortress, a spiritual firewall that silences every accusation and cancels every assignment of the enemy. Your words are weapons.

The Bible says:

> *"And take the helmet of salvation, and the sword of the Spirit, which is the word of God:"*
>
> *—Ephesians 6:17*

When you speak affirmations laced with Scripture, you are wielding divine weaponry. You are piercing through darkness, breaking generational curses, unlocking divine favor, and releasing Heaven's agenda over your life. These are not casual confessions, they are kingdom decrees that shift atmospheres.

And do not miss this: affirmations are not empty rhetoric. They are faith-charged declarations that align your heart with God's vision for your life. When you say, "I am the righteousness of God in Christ Jesus," you are not just stating a fact, you are claiming territory. You are stepping into identity, destiny, and authority.

Even more, affirmations create momentum. They are contagious. When you affirm yourself boldly in God's truth, you inspire those around you to do the same. You cultivate a culture of courage, a climate of belief, and a community where breakthrough becomes normal. This is how revival starts, with one woman bold enough to speak what God is saying.

So, daughter of the Most High, let today be the day you take your words seriously. Let today be the day you choose to speak life, not death, faith, not fear, abundance, not lack. Let today be the day you affirm God's truth with fire in your belly and authority in your voice.

You are capable. You are chosen. You are worthy. You are rising. You were born for this. Now open your mouth, and declare what God has already decreed!

How to Find Affirmations in God's Word

Daughter of the King, the Word of God is not merely a book, it is a living wellspring of identity, purpose, and power. Every verse is a declaration. Every promise is a proclamation. Within the pages of Scripture lie divine affirmations, Heaven-sent truths, crafted to shape your mindset, awaken your spirit, and align your destiny with the will of God.

In a culture that constantly assaults our identity with messages of inadequacy, comparison, and confusion, you must make a divine decision to root yourself in the unchanging, infallible, and eternal Word of God. His Word is not just a comfort, it is your compass, your cornerstone, your covenant anchor.

When the world tells you you are not enough, God's Word declares you are more than enough through Christ. When society tries to redefine who you are, the Scriptures reaffirm whose you are, a daughter of the Most High God, fearfully and wonderfully made, handpicked and set apart for such a time as this.

To ground yourself in God's Word is to anchor your identity in truth that cannot be shaken. It is not a one-time act, it is a spiritual discipline, a prophetic practice, and a faith-building strategy. As you meditate on His promises, as you speak His truth over your life, your thoughts begin to align with Heaven's reality. You rise in confidence, walk in divine strength, and operate with a renewed sense of purpose.

Let's be real: the battlefield is in your mind. Self-doubt is a fog, a shadowy mist that clouds your vision and whispers lies that you are unqualified, undeserving, and incapable. But God's Word is light. It is truth. And your affirmations are the switch that flips the light on.

Every time you declare, "I am fearfully and wonderfully made," you are not just encouraging yourself, you are dismantling demonic strongholds. You are replacing doubt with faith, fear with boldness, and insecurity with Kingdom confidence.

You see, affirmations are more than motivational quotes, again they are divine decrees. When grounded in Scripture, they become a spiritual force that reprograms your thinking, strengthens your heart, and releases the power of God into your atmosphere. They are how you tear down lies and build a fortress of truth around your mind and spirit.

So, rather than rehearsing the voice of the accuser, rehearse the voice of your Father. Do not dwell on what the enemy said, declare what God has already written. He said you are chosen. He said you are victorious. He said you are equipped. He said you are His.

This is how you slay self-doubt:
You stand on the Word.
You speak the Word.
You become the Word made manifest in your life.

Let's take a prophetic journey and excavate some of these affirmations, gems of identity, waiting to be declared over your life. These are not just poetic verses; they are Kingdom keys that unlock boldness, clarity, and power in your walk with God.

> ***"I will praise thee; for I am fearfully and wonderfully made: marvellous are thy works; and that my soul knoweth right well."***
>
> *—Psalm 139:14*

Affirmation: "I am fearfully and wonderfully made."

Pause and declare this with boldness: You are not a mistake. You are not ordinary. You are a masterpiece, fearfully designed and wonderfully formed by the Master Architect Himself. Every detail of your being was meticulously crafted by a God who makes no errors. Your uniqueness is your power. You were born to reflect divine beauty and walk in unapologetic confidence.

> *"The Lord hath appeared of old unto me, saying, Yea, I have loved thee with an everlasting love: therefore with lovingkindness have I drawn thee."*
>
> *—Jeremiah 31:3*

Affirmation: "I am loved with an everlasting love."

This is not fleeting love. This is not circumstantial love. This is covenant love, unchangeable, undeniable, and unbreakable. Heaven has written a love story over your life, and it is eternal. You are pursued, cherished, and celebrated by the God who reigns over all. Let that love become your foundation. Let it heal every wound and silence every lie that ever told you otherwise.

> *"Ye have not chosen me, but I have chosen you, and ordained you, that ye should go and bring forth fruit, and that your fruit should remain:"*
>
> *—John 15:16*

Affirmation: "I am chosen and appointed by God."

This is not random. This is not happenstance. You were handpicked by Heaven, appointed for such a time as this. You carry an assignment. You were born to bear fruit that remains, to release light in dark places, and to walk in divine authority. You are chosen, called, and commissioned. Do not shrink back, step into your mandate with boldness.

Beloved, this is the power of affirming yourself in the Word of God: it silences the voice of the accuser, dismantles false identities, and resurrects the truth of who you are. Every time you speak His Word, you realign with your Creator's original design. You activate your divine calling and ignite the power within you to live a life of purpose, passion, and prophetic impact.

So I challenge you:
Do not just read the Word, declare it.
Do not just hear the truth, prophesy it.
Do not just hope for change, speak change into existence.

Each day, dig deep into the well of Scripture. Find those affirmations that call your spirit higher. Declare them until doubt disappears. Decree them until your atmosphere shifts. Let your words echo the language of Heaven and align your life with the promises of God.

You were born to live affirmed, appointed, and anointed.

Walk in it. Speak it. Be it.

For more affirmations, see the appendix.

Manifesting Declarations and Decrees Through Your Affirmations

Release Heaven's Authority on Earth

Let me ask you a question. Have you ever spoken prayers that felt like they vanished into thin air, words with no power, no shift, no breakthrough? You are not alone. Many believers struggle to move beyond routine prayers into powerful declarations that change the spiritual atmosphere and manifest God's promises.

But hear me now, daughter of the Most High God. There is a way to transform your prayers into authoritative decrees that command the Heavens and bring forth your breakthrough.

This is the power of declaration and decree, the divine authority God has given you to shape your reality.

The Power of Declaration

To declare is to speak with divine purpose and unwavering conviction. In the Old Testament, declaring was a form of prophetic proclamation and worship, announcing God's truth boldly over circumstances that seemed contrary.

When you declare, you are calling forth God's promises as though they are already done. You are speaking supernatural truth to override the physical realm.

Jesus said it plainly:

"For verily I say unto you, That whosoever shall say unto this mountain, Be thou removed, and be thou cast into the sea; and shall not doubt in his heart, but shall believe that those things which he saith shall come to pass; he shall have whatsoever he saith."

—Mark 11:23

This is your authority in action, declaring with faith, aligning with God's will, and stepping into His power.

Key Principles of Declaration

Boldness: Declare boldly. You carry the authority of the Almighty. Speak with confidence, knowing you are God's mouthpiece on earth.
Intention: Speak declarations with clear intent. Your words are not empty. They are charged with divine purpose.

Faith: Declarations flow from unwavering faith in God's power to fulfill His promises.

The Power of Decree

A decree is a divine command, a royal mandate that demands obedience in the spiritual realm. When a king issues a decree, it is law. It cannot be revoked.

Beloved daughter of God, you have been elevated above every earthly king because of Jesus Christ. You have been given the authority to issue decrees that the spiritual realm must obey.

Recall King Darius' decree in Daniel, unchangeable law that governed the earth. Now realize your decrees carry even greater power because they flow from the authority of Jesus.

Jesus declared:

> ***"And Jesus came and spake unto them, saying, All power is given unto me in heaven and in earth."***
>
> *—Matthew 28:18*

That authority now flows through you.

Key Principles of Decree

Authority: You decree with the power of Christ's sacrifice and resurrection backing every word.
Expectation: A decree is not a hopeful wish. It is a command spoken with certainty.
Alignment with God's Will: Your decrees must mirror God's Word. You are His voice, enforcing His Kingdom purposes.

The Blood of Jesus: Your Ultimate Authority

"The Blood of Jesus Was intentional."

—*Shaasia Nance*

The blood of Jesus Christ is your spiritual passport to authority. His sacrifice has cleansed you, empowered you, and granted you bold access to the Father's throne.

"Having therefore, brethren, boldness to enter into the holiest by the blood of Jesus, by a new and living way, which he hath consecrated for us, through the veil, that is to say, his flesh;"

—**Hebrews 10:19–20**

Through His blood, you stand righteous and fearless, empowered to speak bold declarations and decrees that align with Heaven's agenda.

The Role of the Blood

Cleansing and Empowerment: The blood purifies you and equips you to speak with divine authority.
Boldness in Prayer: Because of the blood, you approach God boldly, unafraid and full of confidence.
Victory Over the Enemy: The blood of Jesus is your guarantee of victory over the enemy.

> *"And they overcame him by the blood of the Lamb, and by the word of their testimony; and they loved not their lives unto the death."*
>
> *—Revelation 12:11*

Your declarations wield spiritual victory.

The blood of Jesus was shed for you. The blood of Jesus has given you this access. This boldness. This is why salvation is so beautiful, so powerful, and so incredible.

If you have never been saved, or if you need to rededicate your life, this is your moment and your season. God has called you out of darkness and into His marvelous light to show forth His praise. He made this possible through His Son, Jesus Christ.

Jesus loves you. He died for you.

Why? Because He saw your value. He saw that you were extraordinary, incredible, and worth it. He gave up His life because He knew that the blood He shed for you would be the greatest investment He could ever make.

He died to cover you.
He died to protect you.
He died to have your back.

The Bible says:

"That if thou shalt confess with thy mouth the Lord Jesus, and shalt believe in thine heart that God hath raised him from the dead, thou shalt be saved. For with the heart man believeth unto righteousness; and with the mouth confession is made unto salvation."

—Romans 10:9–10

If you believe that, just say YES right now.
Say:
"Yes, I believe."
"Yes, I believe what you did for me."
"Yes, I believe you died for me."
"Yes, I believe you rose again."
"Yes, I believe what you have spoken about me."
"Yes, I believe you have a purpose for my life."

If you said yes, Welcome to the Kingdom. Your new life begins now. Move with boldness in your Kingdom assignment. Walk boldly as a daughter of God.

Lift your head. Open your mouth. Speak with authority what God has spoken over you. Let His voice be louder than fear, louder than shame, louder than doubt. Let His voice speak to you, through you, over you, and for you. This is your call to live intentionally, declaring God's promises with authority every day. When you grasp the power in your words, your faith will be activated, your mountains will move, and your breakthrough will manifest.

Speak life. Declare healing. Decree success. Command peace over your household. When you declare and decree with boldness, you align yourself with the Heavenly realm and step into your God-ordained destiny.

Remember: You are a royal ambassador, clothed in Christ's authority. When you decree, it is done. The spiritual realm moves. Your circumstances shift. Step into your power, beloved daughter of God. Your words are weapons. Your affirmations are the keys. Speak boldly. Your breakthrough awaits.

Let your words match your destiny. Open your mouth, anchor your mind, and affirm your identity in the Word that cannot return void. You are not just grounded, you are rooted, built up, and established in truth that transforms. This is your moment.

Speak it. Believe it. Become it.

Aim Shift 6: Crafting a Declare & Decree Affirmation Guide

Step 1: Identify Areas for Affirmation

You have already established your 8 purpose buckets. You have filled them with your purpose goals and written your action steps on your ladder, your divine assignments from God. Now it is time to speak life into each area.

Take time to reflect on:

- The prophetic words spoken over your life
- Scriptures that have pierced your spirit and stirred your soul
- Encouragement that stirred something within you
- Challenges that refined your character
- Verses or phrases that continue to echo in your heart

These are not coincidences, they are Heavenly confirmations and divine breadcrumbs.

Step 2: Write in the Present Tense

Scripture says,

"(As it is written, I have made thee a father of many nations,) before him whom he believed, even God, who quickeneth the dead, and calleth those things which be not as though they were."

—Romans 4:17

This is faith in action. Write with authority:

- "I am growing stronger and wiser with each challenge."
- "I radiate love and kindness because I walk in the Spirit's fruit."

Step 3: Keep It Positive and Specific

Your words are seeds. Plant them with clarity and confidence:

- "I attract divine opportunities aligned with my purpose."
- "I walk in patience and understanding, empowered by the Spirit."

Step 4: Align with Your Values and God's Promises

Ask yourself:

- Does this affirmation declare who God says I am?
- Does it align with His plan and promises?
- Does it activate my spirit toward faith-filled action?

If yes, write it down.

Step 5: Write 3–5 Affirmations for Each Purpose Bucket

Give yourself permission to slow down and sit with it for a few days or even a full week if needed. Under each of your purpose buckets, you will find an affirmation category. Begin to prayerfully and intentionally write three to five affirmations for each bucket. Let every affirmation align with your purpose goals and speak life into the woman you are becoming. Listen for the whispers of the Holy Spirit. Write verses, quotes, or Spirit-led phrases that continually capture your heart.

These affirmations should:

- Declare who you are in Christ
- Confirm your calling
- Align with God's Word
- Stir your soul to action

Step 6: Speak Your Affirmations Aloud

This is where power is activated. Your affirmations are now ready to become faith-filled declarations and spiritual decrees. Take each affirmation and boldly speak it with spiritual authority.

Use the phrase: "I declare and decree…"

Example Declarations and Decrees:

- I declare and decree that I am more than a conqueror through Christ who loves me.

- I declare and decree that I walk in divine health and prosperity.

- I declare and decree that God has a good plan for my life, and I will fulfill it.

- I declare and decree that I am equipped and empowered to succeed in all that I do.

These are not just inspirational words. They are covenant truths backed by Heaven. Speak them consistently. Speak them boldly. Speak them until your atmosphere shifts and Heaven's reality invades your situation.

Step 7: Turn Affirmations into Prayers

Use these questions to deepen your affirmation practice in prayer:

- What does it look like when this affirmation is fully realized?

- How can I express this as a prayer aligned with God's promises?

- What mindset shifts must I pray for to walk this out?

- Am I speaking in faith or clinging to doubt?

- What Scripture supports this affirmation?

- What do I need to surrender to allow this to bear fruit?

- Am I trusting God's timing or trying to control the outcome?

- How can I use gratitude in my prayer for this declaration?

- What obstacles must I bring before God as I speak this truth?

- How can I ask God to make this declaration part of my daily walk?

Step 8: Revise and Refine as You Grow

As you evolve, your affirmations should mature too. Review and update them weekly or monthly. Let them reflect the new faith levels and breakthroughs you are walking in.

Step 9: Create Your Affirmation Toolkit

Keep your affirmations where you can see and hear them daily:

- Morning Routine – Start your day declaring your affirmations aloud with boldness.

- Write and Post – Keep them visible: mirrors, desks, lock screens, journals, phone reminders, sticky notes, audio recordings.

- Visualize as You Speak – Envision success, healing, and purpose manifesting.

- Night Routine – End your day by softly repeating and praying your affirmations, reflecting on wins, releasing stress, and anchoring peace before sleep.

Immerse yourself in your declarations until they become part of your spiritual DNA.

Beloved friend, your affirmations are not just words, they are keys, weapons, and seeds. When spoken with authority, they shift atmospheres, break strongholds, and release divine favor. You are chosen. You are empowered. You are victorious. Declare it. Believe it. Possess it.

Let's go!

These declare and decree prayer starters are crafted to empower and uplift you in various aspects of life, aligning your declarations with God's promises and purposes. Feel free to personalize them further and make them a regular part of your prayer life.

Part 4: Intentionality

Intentionality refers to the quality of being purposeful and deliberate in one's actions. Intentionality means being conscious of your choices and actions, ensuring they align with your desired outcome. It is about acting with purpose and determination. Intentionality requires thoughtful, goal-oriented effort to achieve meaningful results.

Think about it like this: When you're driving toward a destination, you don't just sit back and hope to arrive, you stay alert, follow directions, and make intentional decisions to stay on course and reach your goal safely and efficiently. In the same way, walking in your God-given purpose requires intentionality. It means making purposeful choices and taking consistent action in your daily life to align with where God is leading you.

This is not just about "trying harder," but about partnering with the Holy Spirit in a daily, conscious way. Intentionality creates an atmosphere charged with faith and expectancy. It is where miracles stop being distant possibilities and begin to manifest as undeniable realities. It is the difference between wandering aimlessly and walking in God's divine plan with clarity and power.

Remember the Bible says:

> **"For as the body without the spirit is dead, so faith without works is dead also."**
>
> *—James 2:26*

But works without intentionality lack power. When your obedience is intentional, you're not just checking off a to-do list, you are activating God's promises, declaring His truth, and setting in motion the supernatural favor He desires to release in your life.

CHAPTER 7: BEING OBEDIENT THROUGH INTENTIONALITY IS HOW YOU TURN DAILY DECISIONS INTO DIVINE ALIGNMENT

"Intentional obedience is a surrendered life, filled with power."

—Shaasia Nance

Hello, my well-esteemed, highly valued daughter of the Most High friend, I am inviting you, yes, you, to step into this journey of intentionality in obedience. Stop letting distractions steal your focus. Say goodbye to the busyness that drowns out God's voice. Instead, make space. Carve out quality time with your heavenly Father. Come before Him with honesty, with realness, knowing He hears you and delights when you draw near.

Obedience is not just about following rules, it is about partnering with God. It is walking step by step with Him, moving at His pace, and aligning your heart with His will. When you partner with God in obedience, you are not alone. You have the Holy Spirit guiding you, empowering you, and strengthening you to do what He has called you to do.

In the last chapter, you wrote your affirmations. Now obedience requires intentionality. Do not let them stay as words on a page. Pray them aloud as an act of faith, aligning your heart with God's truth and declaring His promises over your life.

This kind of intentional obedience opens the door to deeper connection and divine intimacy with Him. Let your heart overflow with gratitude, because prayer is not just a routine, it is a transformative conversation with the Almighty.

Remember what the apostle Paul said:

> *"Rejoice evermore. Pray without ceasing. In every thing give thanks: for this is the will of God in Christ Jesus concerning you."*

> *—1 Thessalonians 5:16-18*

Make intentional prayer your foundation. Learn God's heartbeat. It is the best decision you will ever make. It is about seeking His kingdom first, tuning into His rhythm, and moving at His perfect pace.

Your intentional obedience unlocks favor, clarity, and breakthrough. So, stand firm, speak boldly, and walk faithfully. God's got you, and He's leading you all the way.

You Are Called to Be an Intentional Obedient Leader

Listen to me, beloved daughter of the most high God. God has called you to lead, but not just any leadership. He is calling you to lead with intentional obedience. This is a sacred assignment that demands more than natural talent or human wisdom. It requires a heart tuned to His voice, a spirit surrendered fully to His plan, and a willingness to walk faithfully, even when the path is unclear.

You are not here to lead by sight or by your own ambition. No, you are here to lead by faith and divine revelation. Your authority flows from your obedience to God's Word and your alignment with His will. You must choose daily to stop, listen, and move only when He moves. The world may rush ahead, but you are called to walk in His perfect timing. This is your secret weapon, intentional obedience.

I want you to understand this: your leadership is powerful when it is grounded in obedience. Every decision you make, every word you speak, every action you take in submission to God shifts atmospheres, breaks chains, and releases favor. Your obedience opens doors that no human effort can unlock. You are not just leading people, you are leading destinies. Yes, it requires courage. Yes, it requires discipline.

Your obedience is birthing a legacy, a legacy that will outlast you, a kingdom impact that will ripple for generations.

So today I charge you to rise up as an intentional, obedient leader. Let your life be a living declaration that God's plan is greater than any obstacle. Let your obedience be your power, your alignment be your authority, and your faith be your fuel. Walk in the Spirit, lead with clarity, and watch as Heaven moves through you mightily.

You are chosen. You are empowered. You are appointed for such a time as this. Lead with intentional obedience and watch God's kingdom come in your life and through your leadership.

Intentional Obedience Begins in the Mind

So let's dig deeper, daughter of the most high. Your mind is the battleground. Your agreement is the key. It is time to ascend into the next dimension, a lifestyle of intentional obedience. This is not about performance, but about divine alignment. It is not about striving, it is about surrender. It is not about trying, it is about transforming.

The apostle Paul declared:

"Finally, brethren, whatsoever things are true, whatsoever things are honest, whatsoever things are just, whatsoever things are pure, whatsoever things are lovely, whatsoever things are of good report; if there be any virtue, and if there be any praise, think on these things."

—Philippians 4:8

This is not a suggestion. It is a strategy. When you discipline your mind to meditate on truth, you activate Heaven's agenda in your life.

Your thought life becomes a launchpad for the supernatural. You were never meant to live in chaos, confusion, or compromise. You were created to walk in clarity, conviction, and consecration. But it all begins in the mind.

> *"For as he thinketh in his heart, so is he:"*
>
> *—Proverbs 23:7*

What you feed your mind is what forms your world. Obedience is first a mindset before it is a movement.

> *"Casting down imaginations, and every high thing that exalteth itself against the knowledge of God, and bringing into captivity every thought to the obedience of Christ;"*
>
> *—2 Corinthians 10:5*

This is mental warfare. Every lie must be confronted. Every doubt must be dethroned. Every mental stronghold must be demolished by the Word of God. You are not a passive participant in your journey. You are Heaven's enforcer. You pull down arguments. You cast out fear. You silence every voice that contradicts God's voice. This is the realm of intentional obedience.

Discipline is not punishment. It is prophetic preparation. Just as elite athletes condition their bodies, you must condition your mind and spirit to respond to the leading of the Holy Ghost.

Your discipline today is birthing your destiny tomorrow.

Obedience is not about perfection. It is about practice. When you choose righteousness again and again, it becomes your rhythm, your default, your identity. Every time you say yes to God, you become the woman Heaven recognizes. You become one who lives by revelation and not by reaction. It is not about how you feel. It is about who you are. And you, beloved, are a daughter of Zion. You are royalty. You were born to obey God in boldness, clarity, and fire.

Your mind needs a gatekeeper. You cannot always control the thoughts that come, but you can control which ones stay. You are the gatekeeper. You must screen every thought and filter it through the standard of truth. Ask yourself: Does this align with God's promises? Does this reflect Heaven's perspective? Does this thought push me toward obedience or pull me into compromise? The thoughts you entertain will either empower you or enslave you.

You are not in this fight alone. The Holy Spirit is your Helper, your Advocate, your Teacher. He reveals the truth. He releases grace. He reinforces your spirit. When you yield your mind to Him, He aligns your will with the will of God. You begin to obey with joy, respond with power, and walk with precision. Your life becomes a living decree, a declaration in motion, a divine blueprint manifested on the earth.

You are stepping into a new era of intentional obedience. This is not surface change. This is supernatural recalibration. You are coming into agreement with Heaven, and nothing can stop a woman aligned with God's will. Now rise. Think on purpose. Move with power. Obey with fire. Your obedience is unlocking realms your eyes have not seen. Your transformation is Heaven's agenda being fulfilled through you.

You are chosen. You are aligned. You are walking in obedience on purpose.

Intentional Obedience Brings Supernatural Results

You were not created to live by default. You were created to live by God's divine design. Heaven has a rhythm and a cadence, and intentional obedience positions you to walk in alignment with the Spirit of God.

> *"This I say then, Walk in the Spirit, and ye shall not fulfil the lust of the flesh."*
>
> *—Galatians 5:16*

This walk is not about routine religion. It is about relationship. Intentional obedience is not merely doing the right thing, but responding to the right voice. It means following divine instruction, not human inclination.

> *"(For we walk by faith, not by sight:)"*
>
> *—2 Corinthians 5:7*

Obedience often precedes understanding. You may not see the full staircase, but intentional obedience empowers you to take the first step, trusting that God will reveal the next.

> *"The steps of a good man are ordered by the Lord: and he delighteth in his way."*
>
> *—Psalm 37:23*

God does not bless random movement. He blesses ordered steps. Intentional obedience looks like speaking what God has declared, even when your circumstances contradict it. It is choosing thoughts rooted in divine truth when emotions scream fear. It is moving forward in faith when nothing around you affirms your direction. Obedience is not passive, it is prophetic. It shifts atmospheres, breaks demonic cycles, and pulls Heaven into your now. Your obedience is a master key. Your alignment is a weapon. Your choice to walk in the Spirit opens gates to divine strategy.

When you begin living with Spirit-led intention, expect a divine shift in every dimension of your life. You will see prayers answered before you even finish them. Miracles will not be occasional, they will become your new normal. Breakthroughs will no longer be delayed, they will be divinely dispatched. You will no longer chase blessings, they will begin to chase and overtake you.

The rewards of intentional obedience are supernatural and measurable. Favor will find you and elevate you. It will break protocol and override processes to position you for divine promotion. Clarity will replace confusion. Your purpose and assignments will come into focus. You will know what to do, when to do it, and how to do it. Provision will manifest. Unexpected doors will open, unseen resources will be released, and everything you lacked in the natural will be provided by Heaven. Peace will anchor your soul. Even in the middle of storms, you will rest in assurance, knowing that you are walking on water, sustained by the One who called you.

Then comes manifestation. What God promised in secret will be revealed in public. The Word will become flesh. The vision will speak and not lie.

Intentional obedience is a daily decision, but you are not walking this path alone. You are partnered with the Holy Ghost, your Helper, your Guide, your Divine Strategist. He will strengthen you. He will correct you. He will lead you into all truth. As you align your will with Heaven's agenda, you will walk in power, move in authority, and fulfill your kingdom purpose. You were not called to wander, you were called to walk with precision. Every step of obedience unlocks the next level of your destiny.

So rise, daughter of God. Silence the noise. Tune your ear to the sound of Heaven. Move when He says move. Your intentional obedience is Heaven's signal to release the miraculous.

You must understand, intentional obedience is a decision you make again and again, but you are not doing it alone. As you partner with the Holy Spirit, He will guide you, strengthen you, and show you how to stay on course. This partnership makes obedience possible and purposeful.

Enoch: A Model of Intentional Obedience

"And Enoch walked with God: and he was not; for God took him."

—Genesis 5:24

Enoch is a powerful example of what it means to move at God's pace. Enoch was not just a man, he was a prototype, a prophetic picture, a divine example of what it looks like when a life aligns with God's heartbeat. He did not chase influence. He did not seek approval. He walked with God.

Heaven did not just observe him. Heaven responded to him.

Enoch walked in step with the Spirit. Not ahead, not behind, but in sync, in surrender, in supernatural obedience. This is not passive living, this is a prophetic partnership. He moved in a rhythm of revelation. Every step was intentional. Every day was an act of worship and obedience.

This kind of walk demands more than a spiritual routine. It requires spiritual sensitivity. It requires radical surrender. It requires the kind of faith that does not flinch when clarity is absent. Enoch teaches us that God is not impressed by perfection. He is drawn to consistency.

When I made the decision to walk intentionally with God, just like Enoch did, partnering with Him in obedience and tuning into His heartbeat, something in my spirit shifted. My prayer life was no longer about ritual. It became relational.

"And Enoch walked with God: and he was not; for God took him."

—Genesis 5:24

Enoch did not just visit God occasionally. He moved at God's pace daily. His life was a rhythm of relationship, not just religious duty.

As I grew more intentional, I realized I was not just praying. I was learning to follow the rhythm of God's heart. I remember one night, during a time of deep prayer, something unforgettable happened. Everyone in my house was asleep, yet I heard loud footsteps above me, so real, so distinct, it was as if someone was walking directly overhead. But no one was there.

At that moment, the Holy Spirit reminded me of how "the the Lord God walked in the garden in the cool of the day."

"And they heard the voice of the Lord God walking in the

garden in the cool of the day: and Adam and his wife hid themselves from the presence of the Lord God amongst the trees of the garden."

—Genesis 3:8

I felt His presence so tangibly, it stirred something deep within me. That encounter marked me. It awakened a holy desire in me to walk with God more closely, to move at His pace, to keep in step with Him like Enoch did. I did not want to run ahead or fall behind. I wanted to walk with Him, intentionally and obediently.

That night, I said yes. Yes to intimacy. Yes to rhythm. Yes to walking with God, not occasionally, but perpetually. I did not want to live ahead of His voice or behind His will. I wanted divine alignment.

You see, before that encounter, my prayers felt like an obligation. My words were full, but my heart was faint. Once I made the decision to live intentionally, to carve out sacred time, to declare Heaven's affirmations, to prioritize His presence, everything shifted. Prayer became a portal. Not just a conversation, but a consecration, a holy communion.

"Draw nigh to God, and he will draw nigh to you. Cleanse your hands, ye sinners; and purify your hearts, ye double minded."

—James 4:8

And when He draws near, atmospheres shift. Bondages break. Vision comes alive.

The more intentional I became, the clearer His voice became. His peace surrounded me like a fortress. His joy filled me like fresh oil. His presence did not visit, it inhabited. I learned what it meant to walk in the Spirit, not just speak of it.

> ***"If we live in the Spirit, let us also walk in the Spirit."***
>
> ***—Galatians 5:25***

Beloved, there is a call right now for you to shift from occasional encounters to daily alignment. From shallow prayers to Spirit-filled obedience. From doing for God to walking with God.

You are not called to run aimlessly. You are called to walk strategically. You are not called to simply move. You are called to move with divine precision. Heaven responds to those who walk in intentional obedience. Just like Enoch, you have been invited into a divine rhythm, a kingdom cadence, a supernatural walk.

So I prophesy over you now:

You will walk in sync with the Spirit.
You will not run ahead.
You will not fall behind.
You will walk in step.
You will walk in purpose.
You will walk in obedience.
And like Enoch, you will walk in such alignment that Heaven will mark you, move for you, and manifest through you.

Rise up, daughter of Zion. Tune your ear to Heaven's voice. Silence the noise of the world. And walk. Walk with intention. Walk with obedience. Walk in power.

This is your season to move. And as you move, prepare for God to meet you in every step.

How to Cultivate Intentionality in Your Daily Life

Living intentionally does not happen by accident. It requires commitment, consistency, and conscious partnership with God each day.

Here is how you can begin cultivating intentionality in your everyday life:

1. **Start with Surrender:** Begin your day by yielding your plans to God. Ask the Holy Spirit to guide your schedule, conversations, thoughts, and actions. Pray: "Lord, not my will, but yours be done today." Surrender opens the door for divine direction.

2. **Set Spirit-Led Goals:** Be prayerful and purposeful about what you commit to. Do not just fill your calendar. Fill it with assignments from Heaven. Set goals that reflect God's heart for your life, relationships, and calling.

> *"Finally, brethren, whatsoever things are true, whatsoever things are honest, whatsoever things are just, whatsoever things are pure, whatsoever things are lovely, whatsoever things are of good report; if there be any virtue, and if there be any praise, think on these things."*
>
> *—Philippians 4:8*

3. **Guard Your Mind:** Let this be your filter. Be intentional about what you allow into your thoughts. Monitor your media, your internal dialogue, and the voices you entertain. When a thought does not align with truth, take it captive and make it obedient to Christ.

"Casting down imaginations, and every high thing that exalteth itself against the knowledge of God, and bringing into captivity every thought to the obedience of Christ;"

—2 Corinthians 10:5

4. **Create Quiet Space:** Intentional living requires stillness. Make time to hear from God. Even ten minutes of quiet reflection, journaling, or prayer can reset your focus and realign your spirit.

5. **Stay Accountable:** Share your journey with a trusted sister in Christ, mentor, or small group. Intentional obedience grows stronger in community. When you feel distracted or discouraged, accountability helps you stay the course.

6. **End with Reflection:** At the end of the day, reflect:

- Did I move at God's pace?
- Where did I obey quickly?
- Where do I need to grow tomorrow?

This habit of reflection helps you build spiritual awareness and strengthens your sensitivity to the Holy Spirit.

You were made to walk with God, like Enoch did. As you cultivate intentional obedience in your daily life, expect supernatural results. Heaven backs your every faithful step. As we cultivate a spirit of intentionality in our prayer lives, we open ourselves to a deeper, more intimate relationship with the One who loves us beyond measure.

Declare this:

"I am obedient on purpose. Every word I speak, every thought I entertain, and every action I take is aligned with God's perfect will for my life. I walk in faith and intentionality, unlocking the supernatural power and favor that God has prepared for me."

Walk boldly in obedience, daughter of God. Live intentionally. Watch as Heaven responds and your faith-filled words bring forth your breakthrough.

Aim Shift 7: Walking Intentionally in Your Purpose

Now that you have identified your Purpose Buckets, your Purpose Goals, your Ladders, and your Affirmation Toolkit, it is time to take intentional action by applying spiritual disciplines, setting healthy boundaries, and developing habits that align with each Purpose Bucket.

Here is your challenge: Under each of your Purpose Buckets, write your intentionalities by noting one discipline, boundary, or spiritual habit you will commit to with purpose. These practices are your intentional yes to God. Whether it is committing to a weekly fast, setting a phone-free prayer hour, guarding your morning routine, or saying "no" to things that distract you, each decision brings you one step closer to walking in sync with God's heartbeat.

This is not about being perfect. It is about being purposeful. Let these intentional choices become the rhythm of your obedience. Write it down. Commit to it. Partner with the Holy Spirit to walk it out on purpose.

Example Intentional Discipline/Boundary/Spiritual Habit:

FAMILY Bucket Example

- Discipline: Commit to having weekly "family fellowship" time through prayer, worship, and Bible discussion every Sunday evening.

- Boundary: Set a no-phone zone during family meals to be fully present.

- Spiritual Habit: Pray intentionally for each family member by name during daily quiet time.

WORK Bucket Example

- Discipline: Start every workday with ten minutes of prayer and Scripture to invite God's presence and wisdom.

- Boundary: Do not schedule work meetings or answer emails during your set Sabbath day.

- Spiritual Habit: Keep a "God at Work" journal to record ways you saw God move in your workplace or through your assignments.

BUSINESS Bucket Example

- Discipline: Tithe from every business income stream and pray over your business finances weekly.

- Boundary: Only take on clients or partnerships that align with your values and God-given mission.

- Spiritual Habit: Dedicate the first Monday of each month as a business consecration day. Fast, pray, and ask the Holy Spirit for vision, strategy, and alignment.

MINDSET Bucket Example

- Discipline: Speak your affirmations aloud every morning, declaring who God says you are (Philippians 4:8 filter).

- Boundary: Set limits on social media and news consumption that distorts your peace or triggers comparison.

- Spiritual Habit: Memorize one Scripture a week and journal how it is renewing your thoughts.

Now go write your Intentional Discipline/Boundary/Spiritual Habit for Each of your Purpose Buckets.

Part 5: Nurturing

Nurturing involves providing support, care, and encouragement to help someone or something grow and develop. It includes fostering and cultivating potential, guiding individuals with compassion, and offering mentorship. Nurturing is about sustaining growth through consistent attention and care, helping to build confidence, resilience, and strength. Whether nurturing relationships, skills, or personal growth, it requires patience, guidance, and a commitment to development over time.

There comes a time in your journey when you must allow others to nurture you. Yes, you are strong. Yes, you are chosen. Yes, you are called. But even the strongest warriors need refreshing. Even the anointed need affirmation. Even leaders need to be led.

Nurturing is God's way of sending people into your life to water your soul, sharpen your gifts, and remind you of who you are when life tries to make you forget. You were never created to grow alone. Even Jesus had disciples. Even Moses needed Aaron and Hur. Even Paul had Barnabas.

When God sends nurturers, they will:

- Speak life when the enemy tries to silence your faith.
- Pour into you when your cup is empty.
- Correct you in love and call you higher, not out of criticism but covenant.

You will know they are from God because their presence brings peace, their words carry weight, and their prayers break chains. They see what God sees, even when you feel hidden, broken, or overlooked.

Let this be the season where you give yourself permission to receive. To be poured into. To be led. To be covered. To be sharpened. To be loved.

"Iron sharpeneth iron; so a man sharpeneth the countenance of his friend."

—Proverbs 27:17

"That I may be comforted together with you by the mutual faith both of you and me."

—Romans 1:12

Declare this:

"I welcome divine connections and godly nurturing relationships into my life. I receive the mentors, spiritual mothers and fathers, coaches, and covenant friendships that will help me grow. I am not alone. I am surrounded, supported, and strengthened by the ones God has assigned to walk with me."

In this chapter, we are going deeper into how to:

- Recognize the people assigned to your growth and elevation.
- Discern the resources aligned with your next season.
- Lean into divine connections that will accelerate your purpose journey.

Be open. Be humble. Be ready. Your destiny is too great to walk it alone.

CHAPTER 8: SURROUNDING YOURSELF WITH NURTURERS: IS HOW YOU GROW FASTER, HEAL DEEPER, AND RISE STRONGER

"There is a lot of glitter in this world, but there are a few that always stick around."

—*Shaasia Nance*

Hey, my purpose-driven, intentional, obedient friend. We have already established this powerful truth: you were born with purpose, an assignment straight from the throne room of Heaven. But let us be honest, the road to fulfilling that purpose can sometimes feel like navigating unfamiliar terrain without a map.

Here is the revelation: you were never meant to walk this journey alone.

God, in His divine wisdom, never sends you on assignment without provision. He places the right people, the right resources, and the right connections along your path to equip you, to sharpen you, and to call you higher. You do not have to figure it all out by yourself. You do not have to carry the weight alone.

Think about it like this: there are destiny helpers assigned to your journey, mentors, coaches, spiritual leaders, and friends, who are waiting to walk alongside you. There are books, tools, strategies, and training created to unlock the clarity and boldness you need. There are divine appointments, God-ordained moments where someone crosses your path and everything begins to shift.

You do not need to wait for everything to be perfect. You just need to discern what is aligned. Walk with the right people. Plug into the right tools. Partner with the Holy Spirit. And trust that the divine ecosystem God designed for your purpose will begin to unfold as you take bold, obedient steps.

It is time to surround yourself with what strengthens your spirit and sharpens your call.

Let's dive in and activate your support system for destiny.

The Power and Gift of Community

Have you ever walked through a season when the weight of life felt unbearable, when the tears came easily, the strength seemed distant, and you questioned how much longer you could keep going? I know I have, and if you are honest, I believe you have been there too.

Here is the truth: you were never meant to carry the weight of your calling, your challenges, or your battles alone. From the beginning of creation to the birthing of the early church, God has always used people to help people rise. Community is not just a convenience. It is a Kingdom strategy.

When I talk about community, I am not talking about surface-level relationships, group chats, or casual connections. I am talking about covenant community, people who are spiritually invested in your growth, your purpose, and your breakthrough. A tribe that prays with you, warfares for you, challenges you to grow, and reminds you of who you are when the enemy tries to make you forget.

Let us go back to Genesis. God looked at all He had made and said it was good, except one thing:

> **"And the Lord God said, It is not good that the man should be alone; I will make him an help meet for him."**

> *—Genesis 2:18*

That was not just about companionship. It was about assignment. God designed us for divine partnership and relational purpose.

Think about Jesus. Even He, God in the flesh, did not walk His earthly ministry alone. He intentionally chose disciples to walk with Him. Together, they faced storms, celebrated miracles, and endured suffering. He poured into them, prayed with them, and prepared them, not just for community, but for Kingdom expansion.

Then, in the book of Acts, we see the early church model a powerful, Spirit-led community:

> *"And they continued stedfastly in the apostles' doctrine and fellowship, and in breaking of bread, and in prayers." "And all that believed were together, and had all things common." "And they, continuing daily with one accord in the temple, and breaking bread from house to house, did eat their meat with gladness and singleness of heart." "And the Lord added to the church daily such as should be saved."*
>
> —Acts 2:42-47

That is what community looks like, intentional connection, shared purpose, mutual support, and divine increase. They were not just doing church. They were being the church. As they did life together, miracles multiplied and the Kingdom expanded.

So now, let me ask you:
Who is walking with you?
Who are you allowing to speak into your life, your destiny, and your purpose? Are you surrounded by people who nurture your spirit, provoke your growth, and pull the greatness out of you?

As you read this chapter, I want you to examine your circle with discernment. There are people who drain your energy, and there are people who will fuel your assignment. There are people who tolerate your presence, and people who will celebrate your calling. Choose wisely.

Your destiny is too great to walk alone.

The Impact of a Spirit-Filled, Supportive Community

Beloved purpose-driven daughter, never underestimate the transformational impact of divine connection. Your destiny was never designed to be walked out in isolation. God's plan for your life includes alignment with a God-ordained community, people who do not just walk beside you but war with you. People who cover you in prayer, speak life over you, and refuse to let you collapse under pressure.

There have been moments in my life, valleys so low I could hardly lift my head, and it was the community God planted around me that became my lifeline. They interceded when I could not pray. They declared the truth when my thoughts were filled with doubt. They reminded me of who I was when the enemy tried to make me forget. That is the impact of a Spirit-filled, supportive community.

Let us break down just a few of the powerful benefits that come from being part of a spiritually aligned, supportive community:

1. Emotional Healing and Supernatural Strength
Healing flows where love resides. Deliverance is accelerated in an atmosphere of agreement. When you are surrounded by believers who are not just spectators but intercessors, burdens begin to lift and strongholds begin to break.

> ***"Two are better than one." "And a threefold cord is not quickly broken."***
>
> ***—Ecclesiastes 4:9, 12***

God never intended for you to suffer in silence. He created community as a strategy of survival and victory. When your arms grow weary, a God-ordained community will hold them up until your breakthrough manifests.

2. Spiritual Maturity and Holy Accountability
You were never meant to grow in a vacuum. Growth happens in the garden of godly relationships.

> *"Iron sharpeneth iron; so a man sharpeneth the countenance of his friend."*
>
> *—Proverbs 27:17*

You need people in your life who are bold enough to correct you, faithful enough to walk with you, and anointed enough to discern the call on your life even when you forget it yourself. True accountability does not just challenge, it activates. It aligns you with God's will and demands the death of every excuse. It will not let you settle when God has called you to soar.

3. Prophetic Encouragement and Apostolic Endurance
Encouragement is not just kind words, it is divine oxygen. It revives, restores, and reignites purpose.

> *"And let us consider one another to provoke unto love and to good works:"*
>
> *—Hebrews 10:24*

A Spirit-led community does not let you retreat. It pushes you forward. It reminds you that the anointing on your life is too valuable to waste, and the assignment on your life is too urgent to delay. When life tries to choke out your hope, your tribe breathes it back into you with the Word of the Lord on their lips.

4. Strategic Counsel and Prophetic Insight
There is safety in the multitude of counselors.

> *"Without counsel purposes are disappointed: but in the multitude of counsellors they are established."*
>
> *—Proverbs 15:22*

God will often hide your next level in someone else's wisdom. When you are properly aligned in community, you gain access to strategies, solutions, and supernatural insight that will save you time, pain, and detours. In the counsel of the righteous, your path is made clear, and your next move becomes undeniable.

Let me say this clearly: your alignment matters. The community you connect with will either cultivate your calling or contaminate it. Choose wisely. Surround yourself with those who see your purpose, speak to your spirit, and stir your soul.

This is not just fellowship. It is divine formation. God is using community to sharpen your discernment, increase your capacity, and prepare you for the next dimension. You were never meant to rise alone. You were born for kingdom collaboration.

I cannot even count the number of times I have witnessed the life-changing power of being surrounded by a supportive, God-centered community. Life will always come with its highs and lows, but when you have people who truly care, who stand in the gap with you, who lift your arms when you are too weary to fight, everything changes.

So rise, woman of God. Link arms with destiny builders. Let your circle be saturated with faith, anchored in truth, and ignited by purpose. Because in the right community, your potential multiplies and your purpose is made manifest.

How to Build and Nurture a God-Ordained, Life-Giving Community

Beloved of God, let me declare this truth over your life. Destiny is not developed in isolation. It is cultivated in the fertile soil of divine connection. If you are believing in God for a community that ignites your faith, fuels your purpose, and walks with you in truth, you must build it with intention, nurture it with love, and saturate it in prayer.

This kind of community does not appear by chance. It is built by choice. It is forged through alignment with Heaven's agenda.

Let me show you how to partner with God to build a circle of covenant relationships that will carry you into the next dimension of your assignment.

- *Be Intentional with Every Relationship*

Nothing fruitful grows without intention. Relationships require effort, consistency, and investment. You must sow into them with purpose. Show up. Engage. Be present. Join a church community. Connect with a small group. Volunteer. Reach out. Community is created by design, not by accident. It is your job to plant the seeds of relationship and trust God to bring the increase.

- *Serve with Joy and Support with Strength*

If you want to receive from a life-giving community, be a life-giving presence. Serve with humility. Encourage with your words. Pray with power. Offer your time, your listening ear, and your heart. Be the one who shows up when others fall. Be the one who intercedes when someone is struggling. What you sow in kindness and support will return to you in multiplied form. When you give freely, God surrounds you with others who will pour back into you.

- *Pray Together with Faith and Fire*

Prayer builds connection and solidifies spiritual unity. When you pray with others, you invite the Holy Spirit to govern your community. Prayer is not just communication. It is a collaboration with Heaven. It is a weapon of agreement and alignment. Whether it is over coffee, through a text message, or in a weekly gathering, make prayer a foundation. Communities that pray together stay aligned and empowered.

- *Ask God for Divine Alignments*

You do not need many connections. You need the right ones. Divine relationships are assigned by God and confirmed in your spirit. Pray for people who sharpen you, who challenge you, who intercede for you, and who see the anointing on your life. Ask the Lord to connect you with destiny partners who will support you in every season. Divine alignments release acceleration, favor, and covering.

- *Lead with Authenticity and Vulnerability*

True connection is built on honesty. There is power in being real. Let go of the mask. Share your story. Be willing to say, "I need prayer. I need help. I am walking through something." Vulnerability opens the door to healing, support, and trust. In that sacred space, community becomes a place of transformation. You do not have to have it all together to be loved. You just need to be willing to show up.

Let me speak this into your spirit. God is building your tribe. He is sending those who will speak life into your purpose. He is surrounding you with people who will fight for your healing, celebrate your growth, and walk with you into your next level. You may have been isolated before, but that season is ending. This is your time to be covered. This is your time to be strengthened. This is your time to connect.

You do not need a crowd. You need a covenant. You do not need many. You need the ordained few.

So step out. Be bold. Stay prayerful. Be open to who God is bringing and trust that He is surrounding you with a circle that will lift you, grow you, and help you carry your cross and your crown.

Together you will rise. Together you will advance. Together you will fulfill your purpose and bring Heaven to earth.

The Importance of Resources in Fulfilling Your

Purpose

Beloved, purpose is not fulfilled by chance. Purpose is fulfilled by preparation. When God gives you a vision, He expects you to gather provision. Every calling requires resources. Every destiny requires supply. Every God-ordained assignment requires alignment with what Heaven has already released into the earth for your success.

When I think about stepping into divine purpose, I see a journey, a kingdom expedition. No one embarks on a great mission without tools. No soldier goes to war without armor. No builder lays a foundation without materials. No visionary fulfills their assignment without gathering what is necessary for the road ahead.

This is not the hour to walk blind. It is the season to walk wise. God is releasing spiritual, practical, and emotional resources for your next level. You must be willing to receive, to steward, and to multiply what He has placed in your hands.

These come in many forms, spiritual, practical, and emotional, and they play a vital role in helping you navigate the path toward your destiny.

1. Spiritual Resources

One of the greatest resources we have is the Word of God. It is not just a book; it is our map, compass, and guide for the journey. When you are unsure of the next step, God's Word brings clarity and direction.

Prayer is another essential spiritual resource. It is not only a way to bring your requests before God, but it also aligns your heart with His will. In prayer, you gain wisdom, peace, and divine strategies. God desires to guide you every step of the way, but you must stay connected and open to His guidance.

2. Practical Resources

Fulfilling your purpose also requires practical tools. These may include books, courses, podcasts, mentorship, finances, and skill development. These are the bricks and mortar that help you build something lasting.

Think of it like constructing a house. Even with a beautiful blueprint, you still need the right materials and expertise. For example, if you feel called to write a book, you may need training in writing, editing, or publishing. More importantly, you will benefit from connecting with people who have already walked that road and can guide you through it.

Do not shy away from investing in your growth. Practical resources equip you to move from vision to execution.

3. Emotional Resources

Let us be honest. Pursuing your purpose can be hard. There will be moments of discouragement, self-doubt, and even burnout. That is why emotional health is a resource you cannot afford to neglect.

This includes self-care, therapy, reflection, and surrounding yourself with emotionally healthy friends and family who support and uplift you. A mental health coach or counselor can help you process internal struggles so they do not hinder your external progress.

You cannot pour from an empty cup. Taking care of your emotional well-being ensures that you stay strong, resilient, and focused no matter what comes your way.

Remember this truth: God has already equipped you with purpose. It is your responsibility to gather and steward the resources that will sustain you on the journey. When you invest in spiritual connection, practical preparation, and emotional care, you position yourself to thrive and not merely survive as you walk out your calling.

You are not in this alone. God is your source, and He will provide every resource you need. Take the step and be willing to receive it.

Who Are the People Assigned to Nurture Your Purpose?

Daughter of destiny, let me remind you again. Purpose was never meant to be pursued in isolation. You were created for connection, for covenant, and for collaboration. God has divinely appointed people, mentors, friends, leaders, and spiritual allies, who are called to walk with you, push you, and help you grow into the woman He ordained before the foundation of the world.

The Bible is full of divine alignments. Moses had Joshua. Elijah had Elisha. Naomi had Ruth. Paul had Timothy. Jesus had His disciples. Do not believe the lie that you have to do this alone. The right relationships will unlock realms of revelation, restoration, and acceleration.

Let us walk through who God may be assigning to your next level:

- *Mentors Who Have Walked the Path Before You*

A mentor is not just a wise advisor. They are a prophetic blueprint. They have endured what you are walking into. They carry answers for questions you have not yet asked. Like Paul with Timothy, mentors do not just teach; they impart. They stretch you, speak into your blind spots, and activate the gifts buried inside you. Who has God placed around you that carries the oil for where you are going? Seek them. Honor them. Learn from them.

- *Friends Who Feed Your Faith*

Not everyone around you is assigned to your future. You need friends who prophesy, not just pacify. People who believe in your call even when you forget who you are. These friends do not compete; they complete. They intercede. They remind you of the promise. They do not let you quit. They war with you and celebrate with you. That is covenant. That is Kingdom.

- *Family Members Who Support You*

Sometimes, the greatest strength comes from the people who have seen your process, the family who still believes in your potential. If you have loved ones who speak life over you and stand in agreement with your purpose, treasure them. Even if they do not fully understand your calling, do not underestimate the power of their presence, prayers, and unwavering love.

- *Spiritual Community That Covers You*

There is strength in the sanctuary. Your local church and spiritual tribe play a critical role in your development. You need intercessors who cover you, leaders who speak truth, and believers who walk alongside you in faith. Do not isolate yourself. The enemy thrives in separation. Plug into the people who stir your spirit and help you stay aligned.

- *Collaborators Who Align With Your Calling*

God is raising up divine connections for your next dimension. In this generation, networking is no longer just about business. It is about purpose partnerships. Think of Ruth and Naomi. Ruth's future was unlocked through alignment. So will yours. Be open to collaborate. Be discerning, but do not be afraid to build alongside people who sharpen your assignment.

- *Growth-Oriented Coaches and Advisors*

Sometimes, you need a spiritual strategist, someone who helps you see clearly, think boldly, and move prophetically. A coach or advisor can help you break cycles, clarify your vision, and take action. They are not there to impress you. They are there to equip you. Their job is to help you fulfill God's plan without delay.

- *Teachers and Leaders Who Impart Wisdom*

God will raise up voices, pastors, mentors, speakers, and digital leaders, who carry answers to your prayers. Be teachable. Be hungry. Be ready. God often uses unexpected people to deliver divine downloads. Do not overlook the voices that stretch your mind and challenge your comfort zone.

- *Destiny Pushers Who Refuse to Let You Settle*

Yes, you need encouragers, but you also need pushers. People who will not let you stay stuck. People who call you higher. People who say, "You were made for more." They may make you uncomfortable, but they are assigned to help you grow. They see your greatness and will not let you hide from it.

God has already provided the people, tools, and connections you need. Your job is to recognize them, receive them, and steward them well.

Your purpose is uniquely yours, but it is designed to be fulfilled in community. Do not wait for the perfect moment to begin. Take action today:

Reach out to that mentor
Schedule that call with a coach
Join that small group or community
Build new, bold, God-ordained connections

You were made for greatness. You were made for purpose. With the right people around you, you can confidently walk into everything God has prepared for you.

Extra Hidden Resources: What's in Your Hands?

Beloved, let this truth settle in your spirit: You already carry what you need to fulfill your assignment. Heaven has not under-equipped you. God has placed within you, and around you, a treasury of divine resources. Many of them are hidden in plain sight. They may not sparkle like silver or shout like thunder, but they are powerful nonetheless. These are the unseen weapons, the overlooked tools, the quiet provisions that, when activated, will shift atmospheres and open gates.

Spiritual Gifts You have been supernaturally endowed by the Holy Spirit with gifts that transcend talent. These are not simply skills or hobbies. These are divine empowerments, given for Kingdom advancement. First Corinthians 12:7 declares, "To each is given the manifestation of the Spirit for the common good." Whether you operate in discernment, healing, intercession, leadership, or administration, your gift is an extension of God's hand in the earth. When you activate your gift, you release breakthrough. When you steward it with honor, you become a conduit of Heaven.

- ***Opportunities:*** Opportunities are more than open doors. They are divine invitations. God is constantly positioning you for promotion through assignments that look small but carry eternal weight. That job interview, that community meeting, that one conversation, it may look ordinary, but it holds the power to launch you into destiny. With discernment and prayer, you will begin to see what others miss. When you say yes to the right opportunity, you step into supernatural alignment.

- ***Time:*** Time is one of the most sacred currencies Heaven has entrusted to you. It cannot be manufactured, only stewarded. Ephesians 5:16 instructs us to "redeem the time, because the days are evil." Time is prophetic. It either advances God's will or delays it. When you align your time with God's agenda, you become dangerous to the kingdom of darkness. Stop spending your time. Start investing in it. God is watching how you move through your minutes.

- ***Financial Resources:*** Finances are not just for living. They are for kingdom building. Money, when surrendered to God, becomes a powerful tool for impact. First Timothy 6:18 says to "that they do good, that they be rich in good works, ready to distribute, willing to communicate;" Your seed is sacred. It has a name, an assignment,and a harvest attached to it. You are not just a consumer. You are a distributor of divine provision. When you give in faith, you activate overflow. When you manage with wisdom, you break cycles of lack.

- ***Creativity:*** Creativity is not extra. It is essential. You were created in the image of the Creator, and that means you carry divine innovation in your DNA. Whether you write, paint, build, design, speak, teach, or invent, your creativity is a weapon. It reveals God's glory and brings healing, beauty, and strategy into a broken world. What you create can shift culture, unlock hearts, and change lives. It is not just art. It is apostolic expression.

You Already Have It

Daughter of Zion, you are not lacking. You are loaded. The oil is already in your house. The people, the tools, the wisdom, the vision, it is already around you. It is time to look again. What have you been ignoring? What have you been minimizing? What are you waiting for permission to use?

God has planted mentors to sharpen you, intercessors to cover you, and friends to run beside you. These are not accidents. They are assignments. You are surrounded by divine connections and supernatural provision.

Now ask yourself: What would happen if I used everything God has given me, not for my own comfort, but for His Kingdom? That is where transformation lives.

As you rise in purpose, commit to stewarding every resource with holy intentionality. Let your time become prophetic. Let your gifts become activated. Let your finances become kingdom seed. Let your creativity become a trumpet of truth.

This is your moment. This is your call. This is your Kingdom assignment. You're not just building a brand. You're building a legacy. You're building culture. You're building the Kingdom of God.

Aim Shift 8: Nurturing your Purpose: Who & What Matters

Take a moment to reflect and write down the answers to these two important questions under your purpose bucket goals. This will help you identify the people, resources, and opportunities you already have or need to seek out to nurture your unique purpose.

1. **Who can help you nurture your purpose?** Write down the names or types of people who encourage, support, mentor, or challenge you to grow into your God-given purpose. Examples might include mentors, friends, family members, coaches, church leaders, or collaborators.

2. What resources and opportunities do you have or need to nurture your purpose? List the tools, gifts, opportunities, and practical resources that can help you fulfill your calling.

This might include spiritual gifts, time, financial support, training, books, workshops, creative talents, or open doors.

Use this simple exercise regularly to keep track of your support system and the resources God has provided to help you thrive in your purpose. Remember, nurturing your purpose is a journey, you do not have to do it alone!

As you create these lists, think deeply about how God has specifically placed these people and resources in your life. Remember, He uses others to support your growth, and every resource, whether tangible or relational, can be used to help you fulfill your purpose.

Take time to express gratitude for these blessings and let them inspire you as you move forward with intention and faith.

CONCLUSION

My purpose-driven friend, I leave you with these words.

Believe God, and MOVE.

- *M – Manifest the Mission:*

You are not here by accident. God has placed purpose in your hands. Manifest what He has spoken over you with courage and clarity. This is your moment to reveal what has been hidden.

- *O – Obey with Boldness*

Step out in radical faith. Obey God's voice even when it challenges your comfort zone. Obedience is not hesitation. It is acceleration.

- *V – Victorious by Faith*

You are not fighting for victory. You are moving from it. Faith makes you fearless. When you rise in obedience, the enemy has to bow. You do not retreat. You reign.

- *E – Empowered by the Holy Spirit*

The same Spirit that raised Christ from the dead lives in you. You are not moving in your own strength. You are backed by the full force of Heaven. Empowered to speak. Empowered to shift. Empowered to MOVE.

Move with expectation. Expect open doors, divine appointments, and miraculous outcomes.

APPENDIX AFFIRMATIONS: BEAUTIFUL AFFIRMATIONS FOR THE JOURNEY

Here is a list of powerful godly affirmations that reflect your true identity, inherent worth, and divine purpose as a beloved child of God. These affirmations are meant to serve as a foundation for building your personal tool kit of encouragement, strength, and faith. You can use them to remind yourself of God's truth, reinforce your confidence in His promises, and align your life with His plan for you.

These affirmations are organized by different categories to help you focus on specific areas of your life. Whether you are seeking healing, confidence, or a deeper connection with God, these affirmations can speak to your heart and guide you through various seasons of your journey. By regularly speaking these truths over your life, you are aligning yourself with God's Word and empowering yourself to live out your purpose with clarity, courage, and peace.

Consider these affirmations as daily reminders of who you are in Christ, how deeply you are loved, and the unshakable foundation you stand upon. As you incorporate these into your routine, you will cultivate a mindset that reflects the fullness of God's promises, and you will be better equipped to navigate life's challenges with a renewed sense of identity and purpose.

Here is a list of powerful godly affirmations, each paired with supporting scripture, reflecting your identity, worth, and purpose as a beloved child of God. These affirmations will help you build your tool kit of faith and strength as you walk out your purpose.

Godly Affirmations

These affirmations are like spiritual truths that you can declare over your life, reinforcing your identity and purpose in Christ. Allow them to sink deep into your heart and mind, reminding you of who you are and whose you are as a beloved child of God.

I am fearfully and wonderfully made by the Creator of the universe.

"I will praise thee; for I am fearfully and wonderfully made: marvellous are thy works; and that my soul knoweth right well."
—Psalm 139:14

I am deeply loved and cherished by my Heavenly Father.

"Behold, what manner of love the Father hath bestowed upon us, that we should be called the sons of God: therefore the world knoweth us not, because it knew him not."
—1 John 3:1

I am chosen and appointed by God for a specific purpose and calling.

"Ye have not chosen me, but I have chosen you, and ordained you, that ye should go and bring forth fruit, and that your fruit should remain: that whatsoever ye shall ask of the Father in my name, he may give it you."
—John 15:16

I am forgiven and redeemed through the blood of Jesus Christ.

"In whom we have redemption through his blood, the forgiveness of sins, according to the riches of his grace"
—Ephesians 1:7

I am a new creation in Christ, old things have passed away, and all things have become new."

"Therefore if any man be in Christ, he is a new creature: old things are passed away; behold, all things are become new."
—2 Corinthians 5:17

I am more than a conqueror through Him who loves me.

"Nay, in all these things we are more than conquerors through him that loved us."
—Romans 8:37

I am an overcomer by the power of the Holy Spirit living within me.

"Ye are of God, little children, and have overcome them: because greater is he that is in you, than he that is in the world."
—1 John 4:4

I am filled with peace that surpasses all understanding, guarding my heart and mind in Christ Jesus.

"And the peace of God, which passeth all understanding, shall keep your hearts and minds through Christ Jesus."
—Philippians 4:7

I am blessed with every spiritual blessing in the heavenly realms.

"Blessed be the God and Father of our Lord Jesus Christ, who hath blessed us with all spiritual blessings in heavenly places in Christ"
—Ephesians 1:3

I am equipped with everything I need to fulfill God's purpose for my life.

"According as his divine power hath given unto us all things that pertain unto life and godliness, through the knowledge of him that hath called us to glory and virtue"
—2 Peter 1:3

I am a vessel of God's grace and a beacon of His light in the world.

"Ye are the light of the world. A city that is set on an hill cannot be hid."

—Matthew 5:14

I am walking in victory and abundance, for God has plans to prosper me and not to harm me.

"For I know the thoughts that I think toward you, saith the Lord, thoughts of peace, and not of evil, to give you an expected end."

—Jeremiah 29:11

I am called to live a life of faith, hope, and love, trusting in God's unfailing promises.

"And now abideth faith, hope, charity, these three; but the greatest of these is charity."

—1 Corinthians 13:13

I am surrounded by God's favor and goodness all the days of my life.

"Surely goodness and mercy shall follow me all the days of my life: and I will dwell in the house of the Lord for ever."

—Psalm 23:6

I am empowered to overcome every obstacle and adversity through Christ who strengthens me.

"I can do all things through Christ which strengtheneth me."

—Philippians 4:13

I am deeply rooted and grounded in God's love, which surpasses all knowledge.

"That Christ may dwell in your hearts by faith; that ye, being rooted and grounded in love, may be able to comprehend with all saints what is the breadth, and length, and depth, and height"
—Ephesians 3:17–18

I am an ambassador for Christ, representing His kingdom and sharing His message of reconciliation.

"Now then we are ambassadors for Christ, as though God did beseech you by us: we pray you in Christ's stead, be ye reconciled to God."
—2 Corinthians 5:20

I am a co-heir with Christ, sharing in His inheritance of eternal life.

"And if children, then heirs; heirs of God, and joint-heirs with Christ; if so be that we suffer with him, that we may be also glorified together."
—Romans 8:17

I am accepted and beloved in the beloved Son of God, chosen before the foundation of the world.

"According as he hath chosen us in him before the foundation of the world, that we should be holy and without blame before him in love: having predestinated us unto the adoption of children by Jesus Christ to himself, according to the good pleasure of his will"
—Ephesians 1:4–5

I am called to walk in humility and grace, showing kindness and compassion to others.

"With all lowliness and meekness, with longsuffering, forbearing one another in love"
—Ephesians 4:2

I am an instrument of peace, bringing reconciliation and healing wherever I go.

"Blessed are the peacemakers: for they shall be called the children of God."
—Matthew 5:9

I am set apart for God's purposes, sanctified and made holy by His Spirit.

"Therefore if any man be in Christ, he is a new creature: old things are passed away; behold, all things are become new."
—2 Corinthians 5:17

I am a temple of the Holy Spirit, and God dwells in me.

"What? know ye not that your body is the temple of the Holy Ghost which is in you, which ye have of God, and ye are not your own?"
—1 Corinthians 6:19

I am led by the Spirit of God, who guides me into all truth and righteousness.

"Howbeit when he, the Spirit of truth, is come, he will guide you into all truth: for he shall not speak of himself; but whatsoever he shall hear, that shall he speak: and he will shew you things to come."
—John 16:13

I am secure in God's faithfulness, knowing that He will never leave me nor forsake me.

"Let your conversation be without covetousness; and be content with such things as ye have: for he hath said, I will never leave thee, nor forsake thee."
—Hebrews 13:5

I am anointed by God for such a time as this, to fulfill His divine assignments and purposes.

"The Spirit of the Lord is upon me, because he hath anointed me to preach the gospel to the poor; he hath sent me to heal the brokenhearted, to preach deliverance to the captives, and recovering of sight to the blind, to set at liberty them that are bruised"
—Luke 4:18

I am a bearer of God's light, shining brightly in the darkness and pointing others to Him.

"Ye are the light of the world. A city that is set on an hill cannot be hid."
—Matthew 5:14

I am strengthened with power in my inner being, through Christ who lives in me.

"That he would grant you, according to the riches of his glory, to be strengthened with might by his Spirit in the inner man"
—Ephesians 3:16

I am a disciple of Jesus Christ, learning from Him and following His teachings.

"Then said Jesus unto his disciples, If any man will come after me, let him deny himself, and take up his cross, and follow me."
—Matthew 16:24

I am called to bear fruit that will last, impacting generations for the glory of God.

"Herein is my Father glorified, that ye bear much fruit; so shall ye be my disciples."
—John 15:8

I am covered by the blood of Jesus, cleansed from all sin and guilt.

"But if we walk in the light, as he is in the light, we have fellowship one with another, and the blood of Jesus Christ his Son cleanseth us from all sin."
—1 John 1:7

I am seated with Christ in heavenly places, far above all powers and principalities.

"And hath raised us up together, and made us sit together in heavenly places in Christ Jesus"
—Ephesians 2:6

I am a partaker of God's divine nature, sharing in His holiness and righteousness.

"Whereby are given unto us exceeding great and precious promises: that by these ye might be partakers of the divine nature, having escaped the corruption that is in the world through lust."
—2 Peter 1:4

I am blessed to be a blessing, sharing God's goodness and grace with others.

"And I will make of thee a great nation, and I will bless thee, and make thy name great; and thou shalt be a blessing"
—Genesis 12:2

I am a witness of God's mighty works and miracles, testifying to His greatness.

"But ye shall receive power, after that the Holy Ghost is come upon you: and ye shall be witnesses unto me both in Jerusalem, and in all Judaea, and in Samaria, and unto the uttermost part of the earth."
—Acts 1:8

I am strengthened by the joy of the Lord, which is my strength in every circumstance.

"Then he said unto them, Go your way, eat the fat, and drink the sweet, and send portions unto them for whom nothing is prepared: for this day is holy unto our Lord: neither be ye sorry; for the joy of the Lord is your strength."
—Nehemiah 8:10

I am a peacemaker, bringing harmony and unity wherever I go.

"Blessed are the peacemakers: for they shall be called the children of God."
—Matthew 5:9

I am called to walk in wisdom and discernment, making godly decisions.

"If any of you lack wisdom, let him ask of God, that giveth to all men liberally, and upbraideth not; and it shall be given him."
—James 1:5

I am an encourager, lifting others up with words of faith and hope.

"Wherefore comfort yourselves together, and edify one another, even as also ye do."
—1 Thessalonians 5:11

I am a warrior in spiritual battles, equipped with the full armor of God.

"Put on the whole armour of God, that ye may be able to stand against the wiles of the devil."
—Ephesians 6:11

I am a steward of God's gifts and resources, using them wisely for His kingdom.

"As every man hath received the gift, even so minister the same one to another, as good stewards of the manifold grace of God."
—1 Peter 4:10

I am a seeker of God's presence, longing to know Him more deeply.

"And ye shall seek me, and find me, when ye shall search for me with all your heart."
—Jeremiah 29:13

I am a disciple-maker, sharing the gospel and making disciples of all nations.

"Go ye therefore, and teach all nations, baptizing them in the name of the Father, and of the Son, and of the Holy Ghost"
—Matthew 28:19

I am an heir of eternal life, secured by the promise of God's unchanging love.

"And if children, then heirs; heirs of God, and joint-heirs with Christ; if so be that we suffer with him, that we may be also glorified together."
—Romans 8:17

Wealth Affirmations

These affirmations provide a foundation for building wealth in your life. By aligning with God's promises, you open the door to opportunities, wise decisions, and lasting abundance. True wealth is found in your relationship with God.

I believe in God's promise that He will supply all my needs according to His riches in glory in Christ Jesus.

"But my God shall supply all your need according to his riches in glory by Christ Jesus."
—Philippians 4:19

I am a steward of God's resources, faithfully managing what He has entrusted to me.

"He that is faithful in that which is least is faithful also in much: and he that is unjust in the least is unjust also in much."
—Luke 16:10

I declare that the blessing of the Lord makes me rich, and He adds no sorrow with it.

"The blessing of the Lord, it maketh rich, and he addeth no sorrow with it."
—Proverbs 10:22

I seek first the kingdom of God and His righteousness, trusting that all these things, my needs and desires, will be added to me.

"But seek ye first the kingdom of God, and his righteousness; and all these things shall be added unto you."
—Matthew 6:33

I am diligent in my work, knowing that it will bring me before kings and not ordinary men.

"Seest thou a man diligent in his business? he shall stand before kings; he shall not stand before mean men."
—Proverbs 22:29

I honor the Lord with my wealth and with the firstfruits of all my produce.

"Honour the Lord with thy substance, and with the firstfruits of all thine increase"
—Proverbs 3:9

I sow generously, knowing that I will reap generously.

"But this I say, He which soweth sparingly shall reap also sparingly; and he which soweth bountifully shall reap also bountifully."
—2 Corinthians 9:6

I trust in the Lord with all my heart and lean not on my own understanding, acknowledging Him in all my ways, and He directs my paths.

"Trust in the Lord with all thine heart; and lean not unto thine own understanding. In all thy ways acknowledge him, and he shall direct thy paths."
—Proverbs 3:5–6

I am blessed in my coming in and going out, in the city and in the country.

"Blessed shalt thou be when thou comest in, and blessed shalt thou be when thou goest out."
—Deuteronomy 28:6

I meditate on God's Word day and night, and whatever I do prospers.

"But his delight is in the law of the Lord; and in his law doth he meditate day and night. And he shall be like a tree planted by the rivers of water, that bringeth forth his fruit in his season; his leaf also shall not wither; and whatsoever he doeth shall prosper."
—Psalm 1:2–3

I am like a tree planted by streams of water, yielding fruit in season, and my leaf does not wither.

"And he shall be like a tree planted by the rivers of water, that bringeth forth his fruit in his season; his leaf also shall not wither; and whatsoever he doeth shall prosper."
—Psalm 1:3

The Lord delights in the prosperity of His servant, and He blesses me abundantly.

"Let them shout for joy, and be glad, that favour my righteous cause: yea, let them say continually, Let the Lord be magnified, which hath pleasure in the prosperity of his servant."
—Psalm 35:27

I am generous and I freely give, knowing that it will be given to me, pressed down, shaken together, and running over.

"Give, and it shall be given unto you; good measure, pressed down, and shaken together, and running over, shall men give into your bosom. For with the same measure that ye mete withal it shall be measured to you again."
—Luke 6:38

I acknowledge that the earth is the Lord's and everything in it, and the world and all who live in it belong to Him.

"The earth is the Lord's, and the fulness thereof; the world, and they that dwell therein."
—Psalm 24:1

I remember the Lord my God, for it is He who gives me the ability to produce wealth.

"But thou shalt remember the Lord thy God: for it is he that giveth thee power to get wealth, that he may establish his covenant which he sware unto thy fathers, as it is this day."
—Deuteronomy 8:18

I am blessed because I trust in the Lord and have made the Lord my hope and confidence.

"Blessed is the man that trusteth in the Lord, and whose hope the Lord is."
—Jeremiah 17:7

The blessing of the Lord brings wealth to me, and He adds no trouble to it.

"The blessing of the Lord, it maketh rich, and he addeth no sorrow with it."
—Proverbs 10:22

I am not anxious about anything, but in every situation, by prayer and petition, with thanksgiving, I present my requests to God.

"Be careful for nothing; but in every thing by prayer and supplication with thanksgiving let your requests be made known unto God."
—Philippians 4:6

I cast all my anxiety on Him because He cares for me.

"Casting all your care upon him; for he careth for you."
—1 Peter 5:7

The Lord is my shepherd; I lack nothing.

"The Lord is my shepherd; I shall not want."
—Psalm 23:1

I commit to the Lord whatever I do, and He establishes my plans.

"Commit thy works unto the Lord, and thy thoughts shall be established."
—Proverbs 16:3

I give cheerfully and generously, knowing that God loves a cheerful giver.

"Every man according as he purposeth in his heart, so let him give; not grudgingly, or of necessity: for God loveth a cheerful giver."
—2 Corinthians 9:7

My God shall supply all my needs according to His riches in glory by Christ Jesus.

"But my God shall supply all your need according to his riches in glory by Christ Jesus."
—Philippians 4:19

I am enriched in every way so that I can be generous on every occasion, and through us, my generosity will result in thanksgiving to God.

"Being enriched in every thing to all bountifulness, which causeth through us thanksgiving to God."
—2 Corinthians 9:11

I am the head and not the tail; I am above only and not beneath.

"And the Lord shall make thee the head, and not the tail; and thou shalt be above only, and thou shalt not be beneath; if that thou hearken unto the commandments of the Lord thy God, which I command thee this day, to observe and to do them"
—Deuteronomy 28:13

I am strong and courageous. I do not fear people, for it is the Lord my God who goes with me. He will not leave me or forsake me.

"Be strong and of a good courage, fear not, nor be afraid of them: for the Lord thy God, he it is that doth go with thee; he will not fail thee, nor forsake thee."
—Deuteronomy 31:6

The Lord has blessed the work of my hands, and my possessions have increased in the land.

"And the Lord hath blessed thee since my coming: and now when shall I provide for mine own house also?"
—Genesis 30:30

I receive God's riches and wisdom and knowledge.

"But of him are ye in Christ Jesus, who of God is made unto us wisdom, and righteousness, and sanctification, and redemption"
—1 Corinthians 1:30

I ask, and it will be given to me; I seek, and I will find, I knock, and it will be opened to me.

"Ask, and it shall be given you; seek, and ye shall find; knock, and it shall be opened unto you"
—Matthew 7:7

I give, and it will be given to me. Good measure, pressed down, shaken together, running over, will be put into my lap. For with the measure I use it will be measured back to me.

"Give, and it shall be given unto you; good measure, pressed down, and shaken together, and running over, shall men give into your bosom. For with the same measure that ye mete withal it shall be measured to you again."
—Luke 6:38

I am able to abound in every good work.

"And God is able to make all grace abound toward you; that ye, always having all sufficiency in all things, may abound to every good work."
—2 Corinthians 9:8

I have made the Lord God my refuge.

"But it is good for me to draw near to God: I have put my trust in the Lord God, that I may declare all thy works."
—Psalm 73:28

I will not fear, for you are with me; I will not be dismayed, for you are my God, I will strengthen you, I will help you, I will uphold you with my righteous right hand.

"Fear thou not; for I am with thee: be not dismayed; for I am thy God: I will strengthen thee; yea, I will help thee; yea, I will uphold thee with the right hand of my righteousness."
—Isaiah 41:10

I will seek first the kingdom of God and his righteousness, and all these things will be added to me.

"But seek ye first the kingdom of God, and his righteousness; and all these things shall be added unto you."
—Matthew 6:33

Family Affirmations

These affirmations and scriptures can serve as a foundation for declaring God's promises and blessings over your family, aligning your heart and mind with His truth and love.

I declare that my family is blessed and favored by the Lord.

"The Lord hath been mindful of us: he will bless us; he will bless the house of Israel; he will bless the house of Aaron. He will bless them that fear the Lord, both small and great. The Lord shall increase you more and more, you and your children. Ye are blessed of the Lord which made heaven and earth."
—Psalm 115:12–15

I am grateful for the gift of family that God has entrusted to me.
"Lo, children are an heritage of the Lord: and the fruit of the womb is his reward."
—Psalm 127:3

I am committed to loving and nurturing my family as God loves and nurtures me.

"Husbands, love your wives, even as Christ also loved the church, and gave himself for it"
—Ephesians 5:25

I speak words of encouragement and affirmation over my family daily.

"Pleasant words are as an honeycomb, sweet to the soul, and health to the bones."
—Proverbs 16:24

I prioritize spending quality time with my family, building strong bonds of love and unity.

"To every thing there is a season, and a time to every purpose under the heaven"
—Ecclesiastes 3:1

I am patient and understanding with each member of my family, showing grace as God shows grace to me.

"Put on therefore, as the elect of God, holy and beloved, bowels of mercies, kindness, humbleness of mind, meekness, longsuffering; forbearing one another, and forgiving one another, if any man have a quarrel against any: even as Christ forgave you, so also do ye."
—Colossians 3:12–13

I declare and decree God's protection and provision over my family daily.

"For he shall give his angels charge over thee, to keep thee in all thy ways."
—Psalm 91:11

I am a peacemaker in my family, fostering harmony and understanding among us.

"Blessed are the peacemakers: for they shall be called the children of God."
—Matthew 5:9

I teach my children diligently about the ways of the Lord, instilling wisdom and understanding in their hearts.

"And these words, which I command thee this day, shall be in thine heart: and thou shalt teach them diligently unto thy children, and shalt talk of them when thou sittest in thine house, and when thou walkest by the way, and when thou liest down, and when thou risest up."
—Deuteronomy 6:6–7

I forgive and reconcile with family members, extending the same forgiveness I have received from God.

"Forbearing one another, and forgiving one another, if any man have a quarrel against any: even as Christ forgave you, so also do ye."
—Colossians 3:13

I honor my parents and respect their wisdom and guidance.

"Children, obey your parents in the Lord: for this is right. Honour thy father and mother; which is the first commandment with promise; that it may be well with thee, and thou mayest live long on the earth."
—Ephesians 6:1–3

I am grateful for the unity and love that binds my family together.

"Behold, how good and how pleasant it is for brethren to dwell together in unity!"
—Psalm 133:1

I trust God to heal any brokenness or division within my family, restoring us with His love and grace.

"He healeth the broken in heart, and bindeth up their wounds."
—Psalm 147:3

I seek wisdom from God in making decisions that impact my family's well-being and future.

"If any of you lack wisdom, let him ask of God, that giveth to all men liberally, and upbraideth not; and it shall be given him."
—James 1:5

I am a source of encouragement and support to my spouse, uplifting and loving them unconditionally.

"Nevertheless let every one of you in particular so love his wife even as himself; and the wife see that she reverence her husband."
—Ephesians 5:33

I cultivate a home filled with joy, peace, and the presence of God.

"Thou wilt shew me the path of life: in thy presence is fulness of joy; at thy right hand there are pleasures for evermore."
—Psalm 16:11

I am thankful for the heritage and legacy of faith passed down through generations in my family.

"For the Lord is good; his mercy is everlasting; and his truth endureth to all generations."
—Psalm 100:5

I am committed to resolving conflicts peacefully and constructively within my family.

"Moreover if thy brother shall trespass against thee, go and tell him his fault between thee and him alone: if he shall hear thee, thou hast gained thy brother."
—Matthew 18:15

I am a parent who leads by example, demonstrating integrity and godly character to my children.

"The just man walketh in his integrity: his children are blessed after him."
—Proverbs 20:7

I trust God's timing and provision for my family's future, knowing He has good plans for us.

"For I know the thoughts that I think toward you, saith the Lord, thoughts of peace, and not of evil, to give you an expected end."
—Jeremiah 29:11

I am a source of wisdom and guidance to my children, pointing them to God's truth and righteousness.

"Train up a child in the way he should go: and when he is old, he will not depart from it."
—Proverbs 22:6

I am patient and understanding with my family members, showing grace and compassion in all circumstances.

"With all lowliness and meekness, with longsuffering, forbearing one another in love; endeavouring to keep the unity of the Spirit in the bond of peace."
—Ephesians 4:2–3

I am thankful for the love and support of extended family members, celebrating our unity in Christ.

"Be kindly affectioned one to another with brotherly love; in honour preferring one another"
—Romans 12:10

I speak blessings over my family members, affirming their worth and God-given purpose.

"The Lord bless thee, and keep thee. The Lord make his face shine upon thee, and be gracious unto thee. The Lord lift up his countenance upon thee, and give thee peace."
—Numbers 6:24–26

I am devoted to serving and caring for my family with a joyful heart, reflecting Christ's love.

"For, brethren, ye have been called unto liberty; only use not liberty for an occasion to the flesh, but by love serve one another."
—Galatians 5:13

I am rooted and grounded in love, providing a stable and nurturing environment for my family.

"That Christ may dwell in your hearts by faith; that ye, being rooted and grounded in love, may be able to comprehend with all saints what is the breadth, and length, and depth, and height."
—Ephesians 3:17–18

I am quick to forgive and reconcile with family members, extending grace as Christ has forgiven me.

"Forbearing one another, and forgiving one another, if any man have a quarrel against any: even as Christ forgave you, so also do ye."
—Colossians 3:13

I am thankful for the bond of unity and love that holds my family together.

"Charity suffereth long, and is kind; charity envieth not; charity vaunteth not itself, is not puffed up, doth not behave itself unseemly, seeketh not her own, is not easily provoked, thinketh no evil; rejoiceth not in iniquity, but rejoiceth in the truth; beareth all things, believeth all things, hopeth all things, endureth all things."
—1 Corinthians 13:4–7

I am a role model of faith and perseverance to my family, trusting God through every season.

"Wherefore seeing we also are compassed about with so great a cloud of witnesses, let us lay aside every weight, and the sin which doth so easily beset us, and let us run with patience the race that is set before us, looking unto Jesus the author and finisher of our faith"
—Hebrews 12:1–2

I trust God to heal and restore any broken relationships within my family, bringing reconciliation and unity.

"And be ye kind one to another, tenderhearted, forgiving one another, even as God for Christ's sake hath forgiven you."
—Ephesians 4:32

I celebrate the unique gifts and talents of each family member, encouraging them to walk in their God-given purpose.

"For as we have many members in one body, and all members have not the same office: so we, being many, are one body in Christ, and every one members one of another."
—Romans 12:4–5

I am a source of encouragement and strength to my spouse, supporting and uplifting them in all circumstances.

"Two are better than one; because they have a good reward for their labour. For if they fall, the one will lift up his fellow: but woe to him that is alone when he falleth; for he hath not another to help him up."
—Ecclesiastes 4:9–10

I am grateful for the generational blessings and promises that God has bestowed upon my family.

"But the mercy of the Lord is from everlasting to everlasting upon them that fear him, and his righteousness unto children's children."
—Psalm 103:17

I am a loving parent, nurturing my children in the ways of the Lord and guiding them with wisdom.

"Correct thy son, and he shall give thee rest; yea, he shall give delight unto thy soul."
—Proverbs 29:17

I trust God's timing and plan for my family's future, knowing that His ways are higher than my ways.

"For my thoughts are not your thoughts, neither are your ways my ways, saith the Lord. For as the heavens are higher than the earth, so are my ways higher than your ways, and my thoughts than your thoughts."
—Isaiah 55:8–9

I am a source of peace and harmony within my family, resolving conflicts with love and understanding.

"If it be possible, as much as lieth in you, live peaceably with all men."
—Romans 12:18

I am a faithful steward of the family relationships entrusted to me by God, nurturing and cherishing them.

"As every man hath received the gift, even so minister the same one to another, as good stewards of the manifold grace of God."
—1 Peter 4:10

I am thankful for the heritage of faith passed down through generations in my family, rejoicing in God's faithfulness.

"For the Lord is good; his mercy is everlasting; and his truth endureth to all generations."
—Psalm 100:5

I am committed to honoring God in my role within my family, leading with humility and grace.

"He hath shewed thee, O man, what is good; and what doth the Lord require of thee, but to do justly, and to love mercy, and to walk humbly with thy God?"
—Micah 6:8

I am a beacon of hope and love to my family, reflecting God's light and grace in all I do.

"Charity suffereth long, and is kind; charity envieth not; charity vaunteth not itself, is not puffed up, doth not behave itself unseemly, seeketh not her own, is not easily provoked, thinketh no evil; rejoiceth not in iniquity, but rejoiceth in the truth; beareth all things, believeth all things, hopeth all things, endureth all things."
—1 Corinthians 13:4–7

Education Affirmations

These affirmations, rooted in scripture, can inspire and guide you as you pursue education with faith and diligence, trusting in God's provision and wisdom every step of the way.

I am grateful for the opportunity to learn and grow in wisdom.

"A wise man will hear, and will increase learning; and a man of understanding shall attain unto wise counsels"
—Proverbs 1:5

I trust that God will give me wisdom and understanding as I seek knowledge.

"If any of you lack wisdom, let him ask of God, that giveth to all men liberally, and upbraideth not; and it shall be given him."
—James 1:5

I am diligent in my studies, knowing that my efforts will be rewarded.
"The hand of the diligent shall bear rule: but the slothful shall be under tribute."
—Proverbs 12:24

I am capable of learning and mastering new concepts with God's help.

"I can do all things through Christ which strengtheneth me."
—Philippians 4:13

I have a sound mind and make wise decisions in my studies.
"For God hath not given us the spirit of fear; but of power, and of love, and of a sound mind."
—2 Timothy 1:7

I honor God with my studies, using my knowledge to serve others.

"And whatsoever ye do, do it heartily, as to the Lord, and not unto men."
—Colossians 3:23

I am open to correction and guidance, seeking wisdom from teachers and mentors.

"Hear counsel, and receive instruction, that thou mayest be wise in thy latter end."
—Proverbs 19:20

I am focused and disciplined in my pursuit of education, keeping my eyes on the goal.

"I press toward the mark for the prize of the high calling of God in Christ Jesus."
—Philippians 3:14

I trust God to provide for my educational needs and opportunities.

"But my God shall supply all your need according to his riches in glory by Christ Jesus."
—Philippians 4:19

I use my talents and gifts to glorify God in my academic pursuits.

"As every man hath received the gift, even so minister the same one to another, as good stewards of the manifold grace of God."
—1 Peter 4:10

I am not afraid of challenges in my studies, for God is with me.

"Have not I commanded thee? Be strong and of a good courage; be not afraid, neither be thou dismayed: for the Lord thy God is with thee whithersoever thou goest."
—Joshua 1:9

I am patient in my learning journey, trusting God's timing for my growth and understanding.

"To every thing there is a season, and a time to every purpose under the heaven"
—Ecclesiastes 3:1

I seek knowledge and understanding as treasures of great value.

"Yea, if thou criest after knowledge, and liftest up thy voice for understanding; if thou seekest her as silver, and searchest for her as for hid treasures; then shalt thou understand the fear of the Lord, and find the knowledge of God."
—Proverbs 2:3–5

I am empowered by God's Spirit to excel academically and spiritually.

"But they that wait upon the Lord shall renew their strength; they shall mount up with wings as eagles; they shall run, and not be weary; and they shall walk, and not faint."
—Isaiah 40:31

I trust that God has a purpose for my education and will guide me in fulfilling it.

"For I know the thoughts that I think toward you, saith the Lord, thoughts of peace, and not of evil, to give you an expected end."
—Jeremiah 29:11

I am a lifelong learner, continually growing in knowledge and understanding.

"An heart that understandeth seeketh knowledge: but the mouth of fools feedeth on foolishness."
—Proverbs 15:14

I am blessed with teachers and mentors who impart wisdom and knowledge to me.

"Give instruction to a wise man, and he will be yet wiser: teach a just man, and he will increase in learning."
—Proverbs 9:9

I am diligent in my studies, knowing that it honors God and prepares me for His purposes.

"In all labour there is profit: but the talk of the lips tendeth only to penury."
—Proverbs 14:23

I rely on God's strength and grace to persevere through challenges in my education.

"I can do all things through Christ which strengtheneth me."
—Philippians 4:13

I approach my studies with a spirit of excellence, giving my best in all that I do.

"And whatsoever ye do, do it heartily, as to the Lord, and not unto men."
—Colossians 3:23

I am equipped with wisdom and discernment to make wise choices in my education.

"But the wisdom that is from above is first pure, then peaceable, gentle, and easy to be intreated, full of mercy and good fruits, without partiality, and without hypocrisy."
—James 3:17

I am a diligent student, committed to using my education for God's glory and the benefit of others.

"With good will doing service, as to the Lord, and not to men: knowing that whatsoever good thing any man doeth, the same shall he receive of the Lord, whether he be bond or free."
—Ephesians 6:7–8

I trust in God's plan for my future, including my educational journey.

"A man's heart deviseth his way: but the Lord directeth his steps."
—Proverbs 16:9

I seek God's guidance in choosing my academic path, trusting Him to direct my steps.

"I will instruct thee and teach thee in the way which thou shalt go: I will guide thee with mine eye."
—Psalm 32:8

I am grateful for the opportunity to learn and grow academically, knowing it is a gift from God.

"For wisdom is a defence, and money is a defence: but the excellency of knowledge is, that wisdom giveth life to them that have it."
—Ecclesiastes 7:12

I trust in God's provision for my education, believing that He will meet all my needs.

"But my God shall supply all your need according to his riches in glory by Christ Jesus."
—Philippians 4:19

I am a responsible steward of the knowledge and skills God has given me, using them wisely.

"For unto whomsoever much is given, of him shall be much required: and to whom men have committed much, of him they will ask the more."
—Luke 12:48

I am focused and disciplined in my studies, knowing that it prepares me for God's purpose.

"And whatsoever ye do, do it heartily, as to the Lord, and not unto men; knowing that of the Lord ye shall receive the reward of the inheritance: for ye serve the Lord Christ."
—Colossians 3:23–24

I am confident in God's faithfulness to guide me through my educational journey.

"For this God is our God for ever and ever: he will be our guide even unto death."
—Psalm 48:14

I am a student of the Word, seeking knowledge and understanding in all areas of my life.

"Thy word is a lamp unto my feet, and a light unto my path."
—Psalm 119:105

Business Affirmations

These affirmations, rooted in scripture, can empower and guide you as you navigate the world of business, trusting in God's wisdom, provision, and guidance every step of the way.

I trust in God's guidance and wisdom for success in my business ventures.

"Commit thy works unto the Lord, and thy thoughts shall be established."
—Proverbs 16:3

I am diligent and hardworking, knowing that God rewards those who are faithful.

"In all labour there is profit: but the talk of the lips tendeth only to penury."
—Proverbs 14:23

I operate my business with integrity and honesty, reflecting God's character.
"The integrity of the upright shall guide them: but the perverseness of transgressors shall destroy them."
—Proverbs 11:3

I am a wise steward of the resources entrusted to me by God.

"He that is faithful in that which is least is faithful also in much: and he that is unjust in the least is unjust also in much."
—Luke 16:10

I seek opportunities to serve others through my business, honoring God with my actions.

"For, brethren, ye have been called unto liberty; only use not liberty for an occasion to the flesh, but by love serve one another."
—Galatians 5:13

I trust in God's provision for the growth and prosperity of my business.

"But my God shall supply all your need according to his riches in glory by Christ Jesus."
—Philippians 4:19

I am a leader who inspires and encourages my team with godly wisdom.

"Where no counsel is, the people fall: but in the multitude of counsellors there is safety."
—Proverbs 11:14

I make decisions based on prayer and seeking God's will for my business.

"If any of you lack wisdom, let him ask of God, that giveth to all men liberally, and upbraideth not; and it shall be given him."
—James 1:5

I am innovative and creative, trusting God to inspire new ideas and strategies.

"Behold, I will do a new thing; now it shall spring forth; shall ye not know it? I will even make a way in the wilderness, and rivers in the desert."
—Isaiah 43:19

I am focused and determined, knowing that God has called me to succeed in my business.

"I press toward the mark for the prize of the high calling of God in Christ Jesus."
—Philippians 3:14

I treat my employees and clients with respect and kindness, reflecting Christ's love.

"And whatsoever ye do, do it heartily, as to the Lord, and not unto men."
—Colossians 3:23

I seek wisdom from God in managing finances and making financial decisions.

"Honour the Lord with thy substance, and with the firstfruits of all thine increase: so shall thy barns be filled with plenty, and thy presses shall burst out with new wine."
—Proverbs 3:9–10

I am resilient in the face of challenges, trusting God to strengthen me and my business.

"But they that wait upon the Lord shall renew their strength; they shall mount up with wings as eagles; they shall run, and not be weary; and they shall walk, and not faint."
—Isaiah 40:31

I am a servant leader, putting the needs of others before my own in my business endeavors.

"For even the Son of man came not to be ministered unto, but to minister, and to give his life a ransom for many."
—Mark 10:45

I seek God's favor and blessings upon my business relationships and partnerships.

"Let thy work appear unto thy servants, and thy glory unto their children. And let the beauty of the Lord our God be upon us: and establish thou the work of our hands upon us; yea, the work of our hands establish thou it."
—Psalm 90:16–17

I am patient in building and growing my business, trusting in God's perfect timing.

"To every thing there is a season, and a time to every purpose under the heaven."
—Ecclesiastes 3:1

I am a wise planner, setting achievable goals and trusting God to guide me.

"A man's heart deviseth his way: but the Lord directeth his steps."
—Proverbs 16:9

I am thankful for the opportunities and blessings that come from my business endeavors.

"Every good gift and every perfect gift is from above, and cometh down from the Father of lights, with whom is no variableness, neither shadow of turning."
—James 1:17

I operate my business with excellence, striving to bring glory to God in all that I do.

"And whatsoever ye do in word or deed, do all in the name of the Lord Jesus, giving thanks to God and the Father by him."
—Colossians 3:17

I am a vessel of God's love and grace in the marketplace, impacting lives through my business.

"Let your light so shine before men, that they may see your good works, and glorify your Father which is in heaven."
—Matthew 5:16

I trust in God's faithfulness to sustain and uphold my business through challenges.

"Cast thy burden upon the Lord, and he shall sustain thee: he shall never suffer the righteous to be moved."
—Psalm 55:22

I am generous in sharing the blessings of my business with those in need.

"Being enriched in every thing to all bountifulness, which causeth through us thanksgiving to God."
—2 Corinthians 9:11

I am a wise steward of time, using it effectively to advance God's purposes through my business.

"See then that ye walk circumspectly, not as fools, but as wise, redeeming the time, because the days are evil."
—Ephesians 5:15–16

I trust in God's protection over my business, guarding it against harm and adversity.

"He shall cover thee with his feathers, and under his wings shalt thou trust: his truth shall be thy shield and buckler."
—Psalm 91:4

I am a person of integrity in my business dealings, honoring God in all transactions.

"He that walketh uprightly walketh surely: but he that perverteth his ways shall be known."
—Proverbs 10:9

I am a visionary leader, seeking God's guidance for innovation and growth in my business.

"Where there is no vision, the people perish: but he that keepeth the law, happy is he."
—Proverbs 29:18

I am a peacemaker in my business relationships, fostering harmony and unity.

"If it be possible, as much as lieth in you, live peaceably with all men."
—Romans 12:18

I am patient in waiting for God's timing and breakthroughs in my business endeavors.

"Wait on the Lord: be of good courage, and he shall strengthen thine heart: wait, I say, on the Lord."
—Psalm 27:14

I am confident in God's plan and purpose for my business, trusting Him for its success.

"For I know the thoughts that I think toward you, saith the Lord, thoughts of peace, and not of evil, to give you an expected end."
—Jeremiah 29:11

I declare God's favor and blessings over my business, knowing that He delights in my prosperity.

"Delight thyself also in the Lord; and he shall give thee the desires of thine heart."
—Psalm 37:4

Ministry Affirmations

These affirmations, grounded in scripture, can inspire and empower you in fulfilling your duties and responsibilities within your church community, reflecting God's love, grace, and wisdom in all that you do.

I serve my church with a joyful heart, knowing that my labor in the Lord is never in vain.

"Therefore, my beloved brethren, be ye stedfast, unmoveable, always abounding in the work of the Lord, forasmuch as ye know that your labour is not in vain in the Lord."
—1 Corinthians 15:58

I am committed to prayer, interceding for my church and its members without ceasing.

"Pray without ceasing."
—1 Thessalonians 5:17

I use my spiritual gifts to strengthen and build up the body of Christ.

"As every man hath received the gift, even so minister the same one to another, as good stewards of the manifold grace of God."
—1 Peter 4:10

I am a faithful steward of the resources entrusted to my church, managing them wisely.

"And the Lord said, Who then is that faithful and wise steward, whom his lord shall make ruler over his household, to give them their portion of meat in due season?"
—Luke 12:42

I support and encourage my church leaders with respect, honor, and prayer.

"Obey them that have the rule over you, and submit yourselves: for they watch for your souls, as they that must give account, that they may do it with joy, and not with grief: for that is unprofitable for you."
—Hebrews 13:17

I am diligent in studying and applying God's Word to my responsibilities in the church.

"Study to shew thyself approved unto God, a workman that needeth not to be ashamed, rightly dividing the word of truth."
—2 Timothy 2:15

I am a peacemaker, eager to maintain unity and promote reconciliation within my church.

"Endeavouring to keep the unity of the Spirit in the bond of peace."
—Ephesians 4:3

I am a faithful ambassador for Christ, sharing the gospel with boldness and compassion.

"Now then we are ambassadors for Christ, as though God did beseech you by us: we pray you in Christ's stead, be ye reconciled to God."
—2 Corinthians 5:20

I practice hospitality, welcoming others and making them feel loved and valued.

"Be not forgetful to entertain strangers: for thereby some have entertained angels unawares."
—Hebrews 13:2

I encourage and support fellow believers, helping them grow in their spiritual journey.

"Wherefore comfort yourselves together, and edify one another, even as also ye do."
—1 Thessalonians 5:11

I trust God for wisdom and discernment in making decisions for our church.

"If any of you lack wisdom, let him ask of God, that giveth to all men liberally, and upbraideth not; and it shall be given him."
—James 1:5

I am dedicated to cultivating a culture of prayer and seeking God's presence within our church.

"And they continued stedfastly in the apostles' doctrine and fellowship, and in breaking of bread, and in prayers."
—Acts 2:42

I give generously and cheerfully to support the work of the Lord in our church.

"Every man according as he purposeth in his heart, so let him give; not grudgingly, or of necessity: for God loveth a cheerful giver."
—2 Corinthians 9:7

I am a listener and peacemaker, striving to resolve conflicts with grace and understanding.

"Wherefore, my beloved brethren, let every man be swift to hear, slow to speak, slow to wrath."
—James 1:19

I am committed to personal growth, setting an example of spiritual maturity for others.

"But speaking the truth in love, may grow up into him in all things, which is the head, even Christ."
—Ephesians 4:15

I trust in God's provision for our church's needs, confident in His abundant supply.

"But my God shall supply all your need according to his riches in glory by Christ Jesus."
—Philippians 4:19

I am diligent in studying God's Word, applying it to my life and ministry.

"All scripture is given by inspiration of God, and is profitable for doctrine, for reproof, for correction, for instruction in righteousness: that the man of God may be perfect, throughly furnished unto all good works."
—2 Timothy 3:16–17

I am a bridge-builder, promoting unity and collaboration among the ministries of our church.

"Endeavouring to keep the unity of the Spirit in the bond of peace."
—Ephesians 4:3

I am committed to ongoing training and equipping, becoming more effective in ministry.

"Study to shew thyself approved unto God, a workman that needeth not to be ashamed, rightly dividing the word of truth."
—2 Timothy 2:15

I am a servant leader, humbly fulfilling my responsibilities in the church.

"For even the Son of man came not to be ministered unto, but to minister, and to give his life a ransom for many."
—Mark 10:45

I am a visionary leader, seeking God's guidance for innovation and growth in our church's ministries.

"Where there is no vision, the people perish: but he that keepeth the law, happy is he."
—Proverbs 29:18

I am committed to the Great Commission, making disciples and sharing the gospel both locally and globally.

"Go ye therefore, and teach all nations, baptizing them in the name of the Father, and of the Son, and of the Holy Ghost: teaching them to observe all things whatsoever I have commanded you: and, lo, I am with you alway, even unto the end of the world. Amen."
—Matthew 28:19–20

I am a compassionate shepherd, caring for the spiritual needs of those entrusted to me.

"Feed the flock of God which is among you, taking the oversight thereof, not by constraint, but willingly; not for filthy lucre, but of a ready mind; neither as being lords over God's heritage, but being ensamples to the flock."
—1 Peter 5:2–3

I am a prayer warrior, interceding fervently for the needs of our church and community.

"Praying always with all prayer and supplication in the Spirit, and watching thereunto with all perseverance and supplication for all saints."
—Ephesians 6:18

I trust in God's faithfulness to bless and multiply our efforts in advancing His kingdom through our church.

"So shall my word be that goeth forth out of my mouth: it shall not return unto me void, but it shall accomplish that which I please, and it shall prosper in the thing whereto I sent it."
—Isaiah 55:11

Mindset Affirmations

These affirmations serve as powerful declarations of the truth of your identity in Christ. These affirmations will shape your mindset and guide you to live boldly and purposefully, knowing that you are fully equipped to fulfill His will for your life.

I trust in God's faithfulness to give me the mind of Christ, filled with wisdom and discernment.

"For who hath known the mind of the Lord, that he may instruct him? But we have the mind of Christ."
—1 Corinthians 2:16

I trust in God's faithfulness to transform and renew my mind, aligning it with His truth.

"And be not conformed to this world: but be ye transformed by

the renewing of your mind, that ye may prove what is that good, and acceptable, and perfect, will of God."
—Romans 12:2

I trust in God's faithfulness to make me strong and courageous, as I trust in His promises for my life.

"Have not I commanded thee? Be strong and of a good courage; be not afraid, neither be thou dismayed: for the Lord thy God is with thee whithersoever thou goest."
—Joshua 1:9

I trust in God's faithfulness to help me cast down every negative thought, taking every thought captive to obey Christ.

"Casting down imaginations, and every high thing that exalteth itself against the knowledge of God, and bringing into captivity every thought to the obedience of Christ"
—2 Corinthians 10:5

I trust in God's faithfulness to work all things together for my good.

"And we know that all things work together for good to them that love God, to them who are the called according to his purpose."
—Romans 8:28

I trust in God's faithfulness to root me and ground me in His perfect love, which casts out fear.

"There is no fear in love; but perfect love casteth out fear: because fear hath torment. He that feareth is not made perfect in love."
—1 John 4:18

I trust in God's faithfulness to fill me with a spirit of power, love, and self-discipline, not of fear.

"For God hath not given us the spirit of fear; but of power, and of love, and of a sound mind."
—2 Timothy 1:7

I trust in God's faithfulness to help me be grateful in all circumstances, knowing that gratitude transforms my perspective.

"In every thing give thanks: for this is the will of God in Christ Jesus concerning you."
—1 Thessalonians 5:18

I trust in God's faithfulness to make me patient and steadfast, trusting in His perfect timing for every aspect of my life.

"Be patient therefore, brethren, unto the coming of the Lord. Behold, the husbandman waiteth for the precious fruit of the earth, and hath long patience for it, until he receive the early and latter rain. Be ye also patient; stablish your hearts: for the coming of the Lord draweth nigh."
—James 5:7–8

I trust in God's faithfulness to help me focus on the positive, thinking about things that are true, noble, and praiseworthy.

"Finally, brethren, whatsoever things are true, whatsoever things are honest, whatsoever things are just, whatsoever things are pure, whatsoever things are lovely, whatsoever things are of good report; if there be any virtue, and if there be any praise, think on these things."
—Philippians 4:8

I trust in God's faithfulness to make me an overcomer through Christ who strengthens me.

"I can do all things through Christ which strengtheneth me."
—Philippians 4:13

I trust in God's faithfulness to help me be content in every situation, knowing that Christ gives me strength.

"Not that I speak in respect of want: for I have learned, in whatsoever state I am, therewith to be content. I know both how to be abased, and I know how to abound: every where and in all things I am instructed both to be full and to be hungry, both to abound and to suffer need."
—Philippians 4:11–12

I trust in God's faithfulness to bless me with peace that surpasses all understanding, guarding my heart and mind.

"And the peace of God, which passeth all understanding, shall keep your hearts and minds through Christ Jesus."
—Philippians 4:7

I trust in God's faithfulness to have a plan and purpose for my life, plans to prosper and not to harm me.

"For I know the thoughts that I think toward you, saith the Lord, thoughts of peace, and not of evil, to give you an expected end."
—Jeremiah 29:11

I trust in God's faithfulness to help me be disciplined in my thoughts and actions, aligning them with His will.

"Whoso loveth instruction loveth knowledge: but he that hateth reproof is brutish."
—Proverbs 12:1

I trust in God's faithfulness to free me from worry and anxiety, as I cast all my cares on Him.

"Casting all your care upon him; for he careth for you."
—1 Peter 5:7

I trust in God's faithfulness to give me courage in facing challenges, knowing He goes before me.

"Be strong and of a good courage, fear not, nor be afraid of them: for the Lord thy God, he it is that doth go with thee; he will not fail thee, nor forsake thee."
—Deuteronomy 31:6

I trust in God's faithfulness to fill me with hope and expectation, trusting in His unchanging faithfulness.

"Now the God of hope fill you with all joy and peace in believing, that ye may abound in hope, through the power of the Holy Ghost."
—Romans 15:13

I trust in God's faithfulness to help me focus on excellence in all that I do, knowing that I do it for Him.

"And whatsoever ye do, do it heartily, as to the Lord, and not unto men."
—Colossians 3:23

I trust in God's faithfulness to make me persistent and resilient, knowing that perseverance produces character and hope.

"And not only so, but we glory in tribulations also: knowing that tribulation worketh patience; and patience, experience; and experience, hope."
—Romans 5:3–4

I trust in God's faithfulness to make me a vessel of kindness and compassion, reflecting Christ's love to others.

"And be ye kind one to another, tenderhearted, forgiving one another, even as God for Christ's sake hath forgiven you."
—Ephesians 4:32

I trust in God's faithfulness to bless me with wisdom and understanding, guiding me in all decisions.

"If any of you lack wisdom, let him ask of God, that giveth to all men liberally, and upbraideth not; and it shall be given him."
—James 1:5

I trust in God's faithfulness to secure me in His love, knowing that nothing can separate me from it.

"For I am persuaded, that neither death, nor life, nor angels, nor principalities, nor powers, nor things present, nor things to come, nor height, nor depth, nor any other creature, shall be able to separate us from the love of God, which is in Christ Jesus our Lord."
—Romans 8:38–39

I trust in God's faithfulness to make me quick to forgive others, as Christ forgave me.

"Forbearing one another, and forgiving one another, if any man have a quarrel against any: even as Christ forgave you, so also do ye."
—Colossians 3:13

I trust in God's faithfulness to help me focus on growth and progress, trusting Him to lead me into His perfect will.

"Trust in the Lord with all thine heart; and lean not unto thine own understanding. In all thy ways acknowledge him, and he shall direct thy paths."
—Proverbs 3:5–6

I trust in God's faithfulness to make me a beacon of hope and encouragement to those around me.

"Wherefore comfort yourselves together, and edify one another, even as also ye do."
—1 Thessalonians 5:11

I trust in God's faithfulness to help me be a wise steward of my time, using it effectively for His purposes.

"See then that ye walk circumspectly, not as fools, but as wise, redeeming the time, because the days are evil."
—Ephesians 5:15–16

I trust in God's faithfulness to help me grow as a disciple of Jesus Christ, continually growing in faith, love, and obedience.

"So Jesus said to the Jews who had believed him, 'If you abide in my word, you are truly my disciples, and you will know the truth, and the truth will set you free."
—John 8:31-32

ABOUT THE AUTHOR

Shaasia Nance is an empathetic visionary, prolific author, and innovative steward dedicated to nurturing the soul and serving others. She is the Founder and CEO of Godly Beauty and the Godly Beauty Academy, where she equips faith-driven women to embrace their God-given beauty, worth, and purpose. Known as the MEGA Overload Coach, she empowers women to move from overwhelm to overflow, teaching them how to walk boldly in clarity, confidence, and calling.

Shaasia is also the host of the Cocoa with Jesus talk show and podcast, the visionary organizer of the annual Godly Beauty Women's Conference, and a certified Master Ministry Mental Health Coach. With over 18 years of experience as an educator, she holds a Master's Degree in Educational Administration, a dual Bachelor's Degree in General and Special Education, and has been recognized as a Yale Fellow for her dedication to education and leadership.

In addition to her leadership and coaching, Shaasia serves faithfully at her home church, Sons of God Ministry, where she leads praise and worship, coordinates youth ministry events, and ministers through dance and choreography. With more than fifteen years of experience in prison ministry, she continues to share the message of hope and transformation with women

A passionate entrepreneur, Shaasia has launched her own line of haircare, apparel, and accessories, using her creativity and business training from the Joseph Business School to inspire others to pursue their God-given dreams.

Beyond her professional and ministry accomplishments, Shaasia finds her greatest joy in being a devoted wife and loving mother. Her heart is to see every woman rise into her divine assignment, and to inspire them to live with boldness, confidence, and faith.

ACKNOWLEDGMENTS

Above all, my deepest gratitude belongs to my Heavenly Father, my Lord and Savior Jesus Christ, and the Holy Spirit. Every page of this book is a reflection of God's grace, wisdom, and strength at work in my life.

To my husband, Ron, my partner, my best friend, and my greatest gift, thank you for loving me deeply, for standing beside me through every high and low, and for showing me God's faithfulness in the way you love, support, and believe in me; and to my precious children, whose joy, laughter, and love inspire me daily, you are my greatest motivation and the living reminder of why I choose to walk in faith, hope, and perseverance

To my mother, whose prayers, love, and unwavering faith have shaped the woman I am today. Thank you for teaching me to stand firm in God's Word and to never give up on His promises.

To my brother, Marquel, who has supported me with encouragement and strength. Your belief in me has been a reminder of the power of family and the importance of walking together in love.

To my pastors, Ronald and Rose Nance, my spiritual covering and shepherds. Thank you for pouring into me, guiding me, and helping me grow deeper in my walk with Christ. Your leadership has been a source of strength, wisdom, and direction throughout this journey.

To those who helped bring this book to life: MaLisha Scott, for your careful editing and encouragement, Charmayne Gather, for your mentorship and wisdom, Teresa Hunt, for your support, and Tanesha Berry, for your creativity and design. I am deeply grateful for each of you.

Finally, to the Godly Beauty community and every woman who will read these pages, thank you for your prayers, love, and support. This is more than a book, it is a movement, and I am honored to walk this journey with you.

STAY CONNECTED

Your journey does not end with the last page of this book. It begins here. God has placed greatness inside of you, and now is the time to live boldly, walk confidently, and rise fearlessly in your divine assignment. Do not just read the words; act on them. Step into the overflow.

Visit Us Online: www.urgodlybeauty.com

Join the Movement: Step into a community of faith-driven women who refuse to settle for overwhelm. Gain access to resources, devotionals, coaching, and events that will help you grow, lead, and multiply what God has placed in your hands.

Be Empowered: Connect with the Godly Beauty Academy, the Godly Beauty Women's Conference, and the MEGA Overload Coaching Experience. Each one was created to help you break through limitations, rise above fear, and walk in your God-given assignment with clarity and confidence.

Together we are stronger. Together we are rising. Together we are moving in God's purpose. The next level of your life is waiting, and I cannot wait to see how God uses you when you choose to step forward in faith.

www.ingramcontent.com/pod-product-compliance
Lightning Source LLC
Chambersburg PA
CBHW021226090426
42740CB00006B/409